ADVANCE PRAISE FOR
Racism, Research, & Educational Reform

"Sometimes schools work—children learn, teachers teach, and opportunities are created. Too often, this happens in spite of the policy makers and master reformers and not because of them. This book is the account of those in Atlanta who have done the hard work—teachers, parents, organizers. Hearing their voices gives us insight into what it takes to make a difference in the lives of children."

Pedro Noguera, Professor of Sociology,
Steinhardt School of Education, New York University
author of The Skin That I Speak

"I believe this book contributes to current debates in education in ways that few, if any, other current books do. As urban education gets lost in debates about the No Child Left Behind Act and high stakes testing, it is rare to get a look at the fate of actual efforts to transform urban schools. The interview with Lisa Delpit extends the work she wrote about in *Other People's Children* and for that alone educators and policy makers will certainly read the book. In addition, the accounts of actual programs and the problems that researchers and reformers face on a concrete level echo many of the education struggles that I have observed throughout the country over the past few years. What I liked most about this book was the toughness and honesty with which such sensitive issues as conflict, racism, internal inefficiencies in the schools, and the very struggle to keep reform efforts going are documented. *Racism, Research, and Educational Reform* does not provide a formula or panacea and, while sharing successes, confronts failures as well. It is an important work that all of us who want to fight racism and develop effective schools that succeed should read."

Herbert Kohl, Director of the Institute for Social Justice and Education,
and Eugene Lang Professor of Education, Swarthmore College

Racism, Research, & Educational Reform

Studies in the Postmodern Theory of Education

Joe L. Kincheloe and Shirley R. Steinberg
General Editors

Vol. 246

PETER LANG
New York • Washington, D.C./Baltimore • Bern
Frankfurt am Main • Berlin • Brussels • Vienna • Oxford

Racism, Research, & Educational Reform

Voices from the City

EDITED BY
Joanne Kilgour Dowdy
& Joan T. Wynne

PREFACE BY
Asa Hilliard III

PETER LANG
New York • Washington, D.C./Baltimore • Bern
Frankfurt am Main • Berlin • Brussels • Vienna • Oxford

Library of Congress Cataloging-in-Publication Data

Racism, research, and educational reform: voices from the city /
edited by Joanne Kilgour Dowdy, Joan T. Wynne.
p. cm. — (Counterpoints: studies in the postmodern theory of education; v. 246)
includes bibliographical references and index.
1. African-Americans—Education—Georgia—Atlanta—Case studies.
2. Discrimination in education—Georgia—Atlanta—Case studies.
3. Education, Urban—Georgia—Atlanta—Case studies. 4. School
improvement programs—Georgia—Atlanta—Case studies.
5. Urban Atlanta Coalition Compact—Case studies. I. Dowdy, Joanne Kilgour.
II. Wynne, Joan T. III. Series: Counterpoints (New York, N.Y.); v. 246.
LC2803.A85R33   371.829'96073—dc22   2004022827
ISBN 0-8204-6772-3
ISSN 1058-1634

Bibliographic information published by **Die Deutsche Bibliothek**.
Die Deutsche Bibliothek lists this publication in the "Deutsche
Nationalbibliografie"; detailed bibliographic data is available
on the Internet at http://dnb.ddb.de/.

Cover design by Joni Holst
Cover photo by Matthew Weinstein
Author photo of Joanne Kilgour Dowdy by Elliott Cramer

© 2005 Peter Lang Publishing, Inc., New York
275 Seventh Avenue, 28th Floor, New York, NY 10001
www.peterlangusa.com

All rights reserved.
Reprint or reproduction, even partially, in all forms such as microfilm,
xerography, microfiche, microcard, and offset strictly prohibited.

Contents

Acknowledgments vii

Preface
Asa Hilliard III ix

Chapter 1 Interview with Lisa Delpit 1

Chapter 2 Interview with Folami Prescott-Adams
Joan T. Wynne & F. Prescott-Adams 11

Chapter 3 Leadership Is Everything: Investing in
Professional Development
Betty L. Strickland 31

Chapter 4 One Teacher's Journey with UACC:
An Interview with Chinwe Obijiofor 45

Chapter 5 The Elephant in the Classroom:
Racism in School Reform
Joan T. Wynne 58

Chapter 6 Finding the Missing Voices: Perspectives of the
Least Visible Families and Their Willingness
and Capacity for School Involvement
Barbara Meyers, Joanne Kilgour Dowdy, & Patricia Paterson 89

Chapter 7 Poetry in the Middle School Classroom
           Joanne Kilgour Dowdy, with
           Martha Abbott-Shim, Lynn Briggs,
           Florence Hardney-Hinds, and Tracy Woodhall 105

           List of Contributors 127

           Index 131

Acknowledgments

We are grateful for permission to reproduce copyrighted material:

"Finding the missing voices: perspectives of the least visible families and their willingness and capacity for school involvement." By Barbara Meyers, Joanne Kilgour and Patricia Paterson from *Issues in Middle Level Education*, 7 (2), 59–79. Copyright © 2001. Reprinted with permission.

"Poetry in the middle school classroom: an artist/activist and teacher collaboration leading to reform" by Joanne Kilgour Dowdy, Martha Abbott-Shim, Lynn Briggs, Florence Hardney-Hinds, and Tracy Woodhall, from *Teacher Development*, Volume 6, No. 1, 105–128. Copyright © 2002. Reprinted with permission.

"Elephant in the Classroom: Racism in School Reform," Chap. 8, *International perspectives on methods of improving education focusing on the quality of diversity*, edited by Rose Duhon-Sells et. al., the Edwin Mellen Press, Lewiston, New York, 2003 (Volume 82 ISBN 0-7734-6889-7).

Asa Hilliard III

Preface

Truth, wisdom, clarity, hope, courage, liberation, and impeccable documentation characterize this volume, which is inspired by the seminal works of Lisa Delpit and resonates with the themes of her achievement in "Silenced Dialogue," the anchor chapter in *Other Peoples' Children* (Delpit, 1995) which delineates the alienation of educators from the children they serve. Dr. Delpit leaped beyond the texts into the real world of urban public education, catalyzing the work of gifted educators, facilitating powerful staff development, and addressing the hidden context of teaching and learning. The gifted educators here are Joanne Kilgour Dowdy and Joan Wynne, and their colleagues, Barbara Meyers, Chinwe Obijiofor, Patricia Paterson, Martha Abbott-Shim, Florence Hardney-Hinds, Lynn Briggs, Tracy Woodhall, Folami Prescott-Adams, and Betty Strickland. This book extends Delpit's vision by synthesizing the voices of these educators and the participants in the project.

The volume's appearance is timely, as the conditions in the urban educational landscape have deteriorated since Dr. Delpit blew the trumpet and made plain deep and complicated truths. This deterioration is hidden in the jargon of school reform and "research-based programs," among other policy and professional language. Who can oppose "No Child Left Behind", "research based programs," "data-driven school improvement," and other such self-evident actions? As Michael Scriven, former president of the American Educational Research Association, said in his farewell address as president, "We have been busy, 'beavering' away," without having raised our children's achievement to high levels.

What greater crisis than mute children, mute communities, and horror of horrors, mute teachers? What greater crisis than for the potential liberators of children to abandon their responsibility to come to their rescue? What happens when "educators" do not feel the intellect, spirit, and humanity of the children? Who are these educators, cut off from the millions of children? How do they define themselves? Do they have a job or a mission? What greater crisis than to have the true master educators, with great power and success, located on the margins of educational efforts?

The deterioration extends from the surface to the very core of services to urban millions, mainly minority ethnic groups. Their unacceptably low achievement is now expected and accepted with fatalism. How do we assess the pain, fatalism, fear, shame, loss of joy, loss of a sense of efficacy that comes with the burden of working in a culture of poverty and neglect; crushing the very souls and spirits of children, families, and communities? How do we deal with professionals who work in these conditions, who cannot feel pride in the work that they do, acting as mere custodians even as they become victims of school and teacher bashing? How will we address the teachers' own genius, spirit, and humanity while they are being crushed as well?

Go to any urban school system where we find large minority ethnic groups living in poverty, and we will see that, as bad as those conditions have been in the past, those conditions pale by comparison to what is happening now. A seismic shift in the type and quality of services has occurred, largely unseen. We can summarize the changes in the following way.

- Radical changes in top leadership in virtually all urban school systems during the past decade or so have removed minority ethnic groups from work as superintendents and top-level staff positions, replacing them mainly with white males who have no pedagogical preparation as educators. They are ex-governors, bankers, accountants, ex-generals, and ex-federal prosecutors. The rule seems to be that those who have prepared themselves as educators will not be hired, and school leadership is really about efficient management. Yet we have not seen higher achievement with these new leaders in charge.
- The work of educational leaders is largely a matter of choosing from a cafeteria of commercial "programs" for school management and for instructional management by remote control. Large national programs promise no more than minimum competency, using standardized scripted "teaching," supervised by alien program managers and evaluators. School "improvement," rather than high-level academic achievement, is the stated educational outcome. Promised improvements are often 5% per year, until the program moves from a lot to a little less below average. Assuming that standardized test scores, with their well-known limitations, are the criteria, where are the urban education centers of achievement that have reached the top quartile?
- Local community leaders, parents, and communities have been effectively removed from any meaningful role to influence educational aims and outcomes. In addition, the role of some schools as pivotal institutions in the local communities has been ignored and lost. The current paradigm is a corporate one. James Comer, in *School Power* (1980), describes a very different set of goals and approach, emphasizing community bonds and other values.

- Gradually, as narrow minimum-competency attainment on standardized minimum competency tests has become the only accountability tool, we have seen the gradual disappearance of programs in the arts, performing arts, forensics, co-curricular activities, health and recreation, and community outreach.
- Staff development for teachers has become, more and more, learning the robotic use of "teacher proof" scripted recipes, and a virtual disappearance of teacher collaboration and problem solving. Simply put, teachers are not trusted or respected.
- The "achievement gap" between traditionally low-performing students and their mainstream peers has been caused by a "treatment gap," really a quality of service gap. It is a new form of segregation, every bit as vicious as the old one. Effectively, segregation has returned with a new face, as can be seen when we note that the standardized, scripted, minimum-competency, commercial programs are found almost exclusively in low-income minority ethnic group communities.
- Finally two historic strategies for the mis-education of minority ethnic populations seemingly now are being repeated. The industrial education scheme that was hatched in the late 1800s and early 1900s white elite think tanks convened at Lake Mohonk, New York, and Capon Springs, West Virginia, became the model for teaching African Americans and Indians in even the higher education institutions. Needless to say, no Africans or Indians participated in the curriculum design. The miseducation and cultural genocide was conducted by moving the children of native populations away from their families, as far as three states, to boarding schools. This was to insure that their parents, communities, and leaders could have no influence on the children. It appears that an updated version of both of these strategies is in place now. Contemporary conservative think tanks have acted unilaterally, without influence from legitimate leadership from affected communities. As a result, elite private networks have designed and imposed a new education order of low-level education and cultural genocide on communities of poor ethnic minorities through the use of cookie-cutter non-beneficial programs.

The implicit premise of this book is that there are not only missing voices, but these voices also carry vital messages that would enable us to create the excellent schools that the students deserve, that have indeed already been created by some. The UACC showcased some of these in its Educational Excellence Expos.

This book focuses mainly on the Urban Atlanta Coalition Compact, the Atlanta Site of the Annenberg Challenge. Parts of the UACC are still in operation in Atlanta, taking their inspiration from the legendary Benjamin Elijah Mays, deceased president of Morehouse College, and his protégé, educational leadership icon Alonzo A. Crim, former superintendent of schools for Atlanta and professor at Spelman College. Add Lisa Delpit as the grand conceptualizer and leader, to a carefully selected staff of powerful educators, including the editors of this book, and there can be no surprise that many positive outcomes have been realized.

For a whole variety of reasons, mainly political and economic, all of the objectives were not met. Yet amazing things were accomplished in the education of urban teacher leaders, some of whom are already making their mark. Just as important as the achievement of outcomes are the lessons that have been learned and reported here. I know of nothing else in the education literature that covers such important experiences in depth, revealing critical aspects of the texture of living institutions. I know most of the participants in the UACC and knew Dr. Crim well. This is an extraordinary collection of activist scholar educators and community servants. He or she who has ears and eyes should listen and see.

I experience two distinct worlds in my professional life. One is the world of pessimism and about false characterizations of schools and the people whom they serve, especially low-income minority ethnic groups. It is also a world where many who have no solution for the problems of low performance, have the greatest access to policymaking, funding, and leadership positions. Worse, many of these same people have positioned themselves to gain personal fame and fortune off the backs of the children whom they claim to serve without ever having led them to high achievement. To them, urban education is a cash cow.

Privateers abound, not unlike the situation in the criminal justice system. Privateers in criminal justice and in urban schools survive and thrive whether or not the inmates or students survive and thrive. The inmate-student comparison is not accidental. As enormous profits made from services to children and teachers in misery continue to grow, the misery of students and teachers grows. Under these conditions, we need the missing prophetic voices that tell the truth and the voices that chronicle the pathway to success. This book showcases some of the most prophetic truth tellers that we have today. I read every line with a new and growing appreciation of these, my colleagues, about whom I have learned even more wonderful things through this process.

Each of these authors is uniquely qualified to speak to the topics that they address. The book rests firmly on a robust empirical base. It addresses the topic of parent involvement, revealing through parent interviews a fresh perspective on how parents are, indeed, often involved and why school staff may not be a part of that involvement or even be aware of it. In one case documented by Meyers, Dowdy, and Paterson, an African American researcher "ensconced herself at a housing project's community center . . . establishing trust, vetted by a key informant, and was able to record the stories of heretofore inaccessible families . . . tracking down elusive caregivers," (interviewing on busses, intercepting parents at dismissal, and conducting interviews on a walk-and-talk basis).

The authors of the chapter mentioned above shine a light on the conditions that make parents feel disenfranchised. They show how parents often see the PTA as perfunctory activity, insincere and trivial, and, therefore, not an attractive option. "One parent called PTA 'foo-foo'. . . I don't have all afternoon to bake cookies, make spaghetti, and lounge around the school skinnin' and grinnin' in folks' face. . . . She [daughter] needs a spiritual foundation in her life at this point of being a teenager."

Parents at the same school say that they want meaningful involvement. "Parents described 'an awesome undercurrent,' 'a chilly feeling,'" one participant said, "Parents feel out of place in the building, in the meetings, as if they are in somebody's way."

One can only wonder if school staff really want and intend to have meaningful parent involvement. Meyers, Dowdy and Paterson discovered a "village community, a community that saw its mission to back and support their children" in a sometimes unwelcome and even hostile environment, where other educators would know nothing about this community. "You know how to encourage babies? Clap for them, babble on and on about how good they're doing; continually talk to them; show them how to do new things; spend time with them, whatever it takes to give them some attention. That shouldn't stop once they're out of Pampers and spending all day with a teacher. "

Dr. Delpit is correct. "One of the biggest challenges for them seemed to be changing their own negative belief systems about children and families that they served." Dr. Delpit also saw the teacher's sense of powerlessness and operations under conditions of stress. With insight, she noted the hierarchical structure of the schools and the resulting lack of a power base for the teachers. One particular insight that carried great weight with me was a comment about how hard it is for people to work together. That is clearly a leadership issue of the highest priority.

Folami Prescott-Adams illuminated many things, most important of which were the limitations of those who take the lead in helping the foundations. She saw the biggest obstacles to working with foundations in the following way:

> I really hate to say this but I have to say it . . . [it is] their own unawareness of the challenges. They don't really understand all of the dynamics of schools. I won't even say of school reform. I will say of schools . . . funders who don't really have a clue. Then even when something really powerful comes along, the "reform" programs have no room for them. I saw one school's faculty get so excited about Professor B's math program, so excited, an, then, hit those walls where the district says "That's not how we teach math." So again they begin to feel like all "hot air". . . . that you're saying reform, but can you really back it up? You're saying reform, and you want the teachers to make decisions about the types of reform and training support and other types of resource support that they need, but are you really going to be able to back it up when someone at the central office at their district says, "Professor B doesn't use a text book?" I don't think so.

This is quite typical, almost the norm in urban education. Powerful teachers and teacher educators are often rejected, while weak programs are fully funded. In this case Professor B has worked with many schools and districts, taking some from worst to first in achievement, regardless of income level or minority cultural status. That seems to be almost a sure guarantee that he and others like him will be ignored in urban education. I know of no commonly used reform program that even comes close to matching the excellent academic achievement results obtained by Professor B.

Some "school reform" has taken the heart out of the teaching learning process and blocked its return. The chapter on "Poetry in the Middle School Classroom" by Dowdy, Abbott-Shim, Briggs, Hardney-Hinds, and Woodhall is a masterpiece that reminds us of reasons why we are in schools in the first place. We are human beings with a human mission. Poetry well taught can do double or triple duty, touching the spirit, building vocabulary and communication skills, and creating community. A visit to "research-based," cookie-cutter programs in urban education environments will give immediate evidence of sterility as well as low achievement.

Few educators or the general public at large have an appreciation of the complicated context within which schooling takes place. Everyone has gone to school and thinks of themselves as a lay expert. The missing voices should disabuse us of that notion. A few brief examples from the field will reveal the universality of the issues raised from the UACC experience as well as the relevance of the vision of the authors for bringing harmony into being.

Angela Hunter, Oakland, California 4th Grade Master Teacher

Angela Hunter taught a low-income class that became 4th grade forensics champion in Oakland, California. Her class also won first place in a poetry contest. The Oakland Museum selected the work of that class to publish from forty-four 4th grade classes in the district! Ms Hunter was a substitute teacher at the time with no teaching credentials! She had to go to war with the system to be able to apply her unconventional talents, while the school system tried to put her in a box with scripted programs. Happily she refuses to bend. Just as with Professor B above, current structures seem to have little room for success, only profiteers.

Tori Hugar: Houston Master Teacher

In order to give even more texture to the experience of teachers like Ms Hunter, we review the work of Houston master teacher, Tori Hugar, who produces outstanding student achievement, the only definition of "master teacher."

> When I first became a classroom teacher, I felt as though I could conquer the world. I wanted to go back to my neighborhood (an inner-city low-income area) and teach, you know, give back to my community. I wanted to become as compelling and as influential as my teachers were. I felt blessed when I was not only able to work in my neighborhood, but to actually get a position at the elementary school which I attended. My elementary principal and mentor hired me as soon as she got an opening. Her influence in my life is one of the reasons that I am who I am today. She taught me the importance of

an education and followed my educational career to the end, making sure I did not end up a statistic. She gave me a feeling of self-worth, advice, money and she even gave me a swat on my behind from time to time. Most of all, she gave me her LOVE. Her motto is "Knowledge is power," and she always insisted we put the children first. With all that she gave and taught, how could I ever let her down? How could I even consider working somewhere else? The answer is simple. Our school district adopted the Project GRAD programs, and I immediately realized that these programs definitely weren't what were best for the children. Once I realized that one person could not make a difference, I left.

Project GRAD meant lots of changes for our school and our district. I immediately knew the main components of the project would not work for our kids. The first one being Success for All (SFA). This 90-minute drill and practice routine was a daily disaster. Our school already had a very effective reading program called Open Court. My principal knew it was one of the best programs available and held on to it until the last year the district allowed her to. Project GRAD finally insisted we change over.

Most of the teachers did not buy into the program, so one can imagine how effective they were at teaching something they did not believe in. The children read, or should I say called words (Calling words is reading with no comprehension), and the teachers asked questions attempting to get the students to respond. Usually the teachers did most of the responding. Students did not react well to the program because it grouped them according to their level of reading. Although the program was designed so that the children would not know one level from another, the students were very quick to pick up on who the better readers were and who the "slow" readers were. Children are not idiots, and they can tell when segregation is slapping them in the face. They knew exactly what was going on. Did the self-esteem of those "slow" readers drop? You better believe it did. Did they strive to move to a higher level? Well, that depended on the teacher. Some of them were very encouraging to the students, but you must remember the teachers did not like the program. Therefore, their motivation was sometimes lower than that of students. Do our children really need another program that will slow them down? Why do we frustrate our teachers with programs they don't believe in? Shouldn't the schools ask the teachers what they think is best for their students? We certainly do not need a program that lowers students' self-esteem, categorizes them according to ability instead of the strength of their character, and does not allow them to think while they learn.

Houston Independent School District has taken an altogether different approach to reading by including Reading in the Language Arts Department. Somebody finally realized that Reading is Language. Reading is Social Studies. Reading is Science. . . . Reading encompasses all of these subjects and more. It should be emphasized all day. It is not mandatory that each subdistrict buy into this holistic approach to reading. Guess who is not buying into it? The Project GRAD. Children in these districts are, therefore, being handicapped by not being taught to think and understand what they read and hear. They just become "word callers."

Our school housed children from a local women's rehabilitation center. This meant a large percentage of our children were only there for a few months at a time, which is the case in many inner-city schools. "Move It Math" is the primary math program. It is designed for students to begin working on certain concepts in the kindergarten and continues with these same concepts to fifth/sixth grade. It requires the teacher receive at least a week of training that usually leaves him/her confused and needing more training. The district required us to implement the program. So, because we didn't quite get it, we trained the kids to play act when the powers that be came to check on us, and we (the teachers) put on a great song and dance routine that overwhelmingly convinced them that their program was working. The test results prove them wrong, but they always seemed to justify the failing grades in one way or another at the students' expense.

The program uses manipulatives and tons of innovative teaching techniques that would be perfect for children who actually grew up in the neighborhood. How often is that the case? Finding an inner-city student who remains in the same school for six years is rare. Home renters don't usually stay put that long. The students go to other schools enthusiastically talking about "crabs adding," "tractors dividing," "tap and talley," etc. The students' new school would automatically consider these children "at risk" and behind the other children because the teachers are not familiar with the M.I.M. program. (It also doesn't help that the children are minority, transient, of a low-income family, and have low self-esteem.)

I had the opportunity to talk to Mr. and Mrs. Shoecraft (the founders of M.I.M.) at a restaurant. I asked them if they were aware of what their program was doing to the children in these neighborhoods. Their reply was that they had not thought about it from that perspective. Why should they? They got paid for the program and actually have very little to do with its implementation at this point. Can the program work for children? Yes. Does it work for our children? Absolutely not.

There is not a teacher alive who has not had problems with classroom management. All of us appreciate ideas that will help our school day run smoothly. Most of us have some idea of how we would like our students to feel about us and what we would like the atmosphere in our classrooms to be. We don't want to be cloned. The Consistency Management and Cooperative Discipline (CMCD) program is definitely in the "cloning business." Every classroom in every school had to have the exact same things on the walls. Every teacher in every school had to run their classes in the same way. Every teacher is strongly encouraged not to change the building blocks of CMCD to suit their own teaching style. Ideally, the whole school should be on the same page where discipline is concerned; however, teachers should be able to implement their own general routine while in the classroom. Children look forward to a new year with a new teacher. They don't want to walk into their new classroom and see the same "old" materials. Teachers should be introduced to new material and should be allowed to share techniques that work for them. They should then be allowed to pick and choose what fits their personality and teaching styles.

We do need help . . . desperately. We need programs that will empower, encourage, and equip our teachers with the necessary knowledge and skills needed to educate our children. We need programs that offer materials our students can relate to culturally and that promote meaningful parent teacher relationships. We need to fall back on the basic fundamentals of teaching that promote higher level thinking and that lead to success throughout the child's life rather than gimmicks and games that temporarily make the child "feel good." (Hugar, 2003)

Tori Hugar's experiences are needed in order to see the effect of the soul-shattering experiences that our teachers in urban schools must endure. Other teachers with the same potential are rarely exposed to teachers like Ms. Hugar and Ms. Hunter. This may well be both the new segregation and the new racism. It is an intolerable situation.

Dorothy Scott: Master Teacher at Prescott School, Oakland, California

Master teacher Carrie Secret at the Prescott School in Oakland, California, reported in an interview with me in January 2004 about the current experience of one of her peers. Prescott School is in the lowest income area in Oakland and is almost 100% African American. Master teacher Dorothy Scott's 5th grade class at the Prescott school scored 99.9 on the nationally standardized reading test! Now that teacher is the subject of an investigation!

Ms. Scott had taught the same children for three years. On her own, she kept the children after school. Members of the investigative panel asked her if she gave the children pretzels for a snack while keeping them after school. She answered, "No, my husband and I brought fried chicken, greens and cornbread for them."

The lawyer that she retained for her hearing asked the panel, "Have you been in her room?" The response of the panel was "No." The lawyer then responded, "Oh, poor, black, high-performing children, therefore they cheated? Sounds like white supremacy."

Ms. Scott had no student who scored below the 50th percentile in a class of 25. Ms. Scott told the panel that she was disappointed in her own performance because she wanted her class to score a perfect 100. One of her peers told her that as an artifact of the scoring, no class could make a perfect 100. Ms. Scott responded, "Just think, all these years, I have been trying to get 100 and have just now found out that it cannot be done!"

Then the lawyer asked the panel, "Have you held hearings at the high performing white schools? The panel response was "No." The attorney then commented, "Oh, sounds like white supremacy to me." To respond to the panel that was actually challenging her character, Ms. Scott told them, "I still have boxes full of my children's work that you can see." So far, she has had no takers. Sounds like racism to me.

Audrey Bullard: Master Principal, Chick Elementary School in Kansas City, Missouri, and Leader of the Ladd Middle School, Both Placed First in Academic Achievement

Eric Adler reported for the *Kansas City Star* on Audrey Bullard's reward for her excellent achievement, the trouble!

"Shhhh. Quiet. Listen. Listen closely as Audrey Bullard—the longtime principal of one of the most controversial yet successful elementary schools in the Kansas City School District, African-themed Chick Elementary—reveals the secret of reaching kids many others rarely reach. Poor kids. Urban kids. Too many from hard homes. In an office adorned with African totems and art, Bullard sits with perfect posture, her neck ramrod straight, her impossibly high cheekbones held aloft by a large, hospitable smile. For 40 years the Depression-era daughter of a seamstress mom and cotton farmer dad has been an educator. She's spent 15 years as Chick's principal. The Afro-centric theme, in which lessons revolve around African and African American culture, literature, history and philosophy, was her brainchild. And she's succeeded.

Under her guidance, and despite a few Afro-centric education skeptics, many of Chick's kindergarten to fifth graders rank every year alongside some of Missouri's best students on state tests. Missouri's goal for 2003, for example, was that 9.3 percent of the students should test proficient in math and 19.4 percent in English.

Chick's urban students smashed those goals with 38.3 percent proficient in math, 61.4 percent proficient in English. No school in the district did better in both areas, which has made recent high-profile wrangling even harder for Bullard to accept.

Bullard rarely raises her voice. Speaking passionately, her voice quiets to a near whisper, drawing her listeners in. Yet last year, in a fit of frustration, she exploded at a forum before the Kansas City Missouri School Board. The topic was whether Bullard would run a new middle school under the same Afro-centric theme. She thought the issues already settled. So when the board balked, asked for more time, questioned what to name the school, Bullard lambasted the board to its face and in the press. In the end she would be reprimanded and lose her chance to be principal at the school. (Adler, 2003)

Deann Smith, also a reporter with the *Kansas City Star*, reported on Audrey Bullard's struggle.

. . . Besides serving as Chick's principal, Bullard also was principal at an African-centered middle school that opened in August 2002. Chick has some of the district's top test scores, and in July 2002 Bullard received an "outstanding" performance evaluation, the lawsuit says. Last September, Taylor reprimanded Bullard for using her district credit card to buy air-conditioning units for sweltering classes. Then in early December, Bullard was quoted in *The Call* newspaper as criticizing Warrick for her opposition to naming the new middle school after John Henrik Clarke, a deceased African studies scholar from New York. K.C. Taylor sent Bullard a letter on Dec. 19 reprimanding her for continuing "to flout board policy and publicly criticizing the board and administration." She was placed on probation and removed as middle school principal. (Smith, 2003)

Professor Linwood Tauheed of the University of Missouri reported that, although the Jenkins Desegregation case provided nearly $2 billion for the improvement of African American education in the Kansas City School District, and a major magnet school effort was made to bring white students back into the district, at $50,000 per year on taxi fares, no significant gains were made in school district achievement. However, both the Chick and Ladd schools that Audrey Bullard led, which received none of the $2 billion, scored at the very top of the city!

Conclusion

The truths told in this book, and in the master teacher experiences cited above raise fundamental questions about school reform in urban areas. Clearly the culture and mental capacities of our children are not an impediment to their success. It is also true that many educators know how to create an excellent school environment. It is true that political forces are in conflict about the level and type of support that should be given to the schools. It is true that racism is still a major factor in the school environment just as it is in the environment in general. It is true that the large urban budgets have been spotted by the venture capitalists, who control increasingly large parts of educational policy, educational ideology, educational leadership, educational "philanthropy," educational research, and educational media. Finally, it is true that urban education is not a priority in America, No Child Left Behind notwithstanding.

We have to be honest about the world that we occupy. Conflicts in high places continue now as they did when the debate over support for public education began (Cubberly, 1920). A powerful sector of the American elite is engaged in what amounts to an attack on public education (Berliner, 1995). It is very interesting to examine current popular, well-promoted missives on the education of poor children and African children in particular. Let's look at Arthur Jensen's *Harvard Educational Review* article, "How Much Can We Boost IQ?," Arthur Jensen's *Bias in Mental Testing*, *The Bell Curve*, and *IQ and the Wealth of Nations*. This intellectual deficiency argument of African Americans and Africans spans decades, and as the recent publications show, there is no sign of a let up. The domestic argument is quickly internationalized. In other words, Africans in America remain on the bottom because of low intellect. Similarly, African nations remain on the bottom because of a low national IQ. Moreover, it is the current power elite that spawns these texts, e.g., the Bradley Foundation support for the *Bell Curve*, and the Heritage Foundation support for Charles Murray, an adviser to that network for many years as well as co-author of the *Bell Curve*.

The companion argument is also decades old, still supported by the same network, and is also both local and internationalized. The culturally deprived argument was a central explanation for the failure of poor and ethnic minority children in the late 1950s and 1960s. The newest iterations of this argument are the well-publicized books *No Excuses* by the Thernstroms at Harvard (Thernstrom and Thernstrom, 2003) and the international version *Culture Matters* (Harrison and Huntington, 2000).

This argument ignores the intellectual deficiency argument without really repudiating it. It says that African American children do not learn because of their bad culture.

The *Culture Matters* book then makes the same argument about Africa, saying that African nations remain on the bottom because of their bad African culture. The remedy is for the former slavers, present neo-colonizers, former segregators to change the culture of Africans at home and abroad. Again, the same network that supported the IQ arguments is there for the culturally deprived argument. These anti-African ideologies and actions are contemporary, just as they were present in the past.

Slavery and colonization as well as segregation/apartheid are "culture wars." Labeling victims as uncivilized, pagan, primitive, etc., has been and remains a pretext for exploitation. We have not overcome.

This is also the network that does not want public education but wants to profit from public education, if it exists, as Chris Whittle and his Channel One and the Edison Project show [With Success For All now bundled into some of the Edison Projects]. It is also the school voucher network (Edwards, 2000). To my knowledge, they have never produced "success for all." They have only produced financial success for some.

The same network has declared "culture wars" on curriculum content that recovers the heritage of African Americans and others. They have tried to build walls to protect the existing non-culturally responsive curriculum against all challenges. Clearly, the scope and depth of the interest of this network are great. It avoids the master teachers and powerful schools such as those examples given above. For example, the Thernstroms did not deal in their book with the Chick Elementary African-centered highest performing school though they visited Kansas City to get material for the book. It would have destroyed a fundamental premise of their argument to acknowledge a school that did use the "deficient" culture argument, an African-centered public school, one of two that led the city (Adler, 2003; Smith, 2003).

The problems are great and complex. Most of them are old with new names. The same sides from the past are still competing on the field. The good news is that the children were geniuses then and are geniuses now and show themselves to be resilient in spite of the "savage inequalities " in opportunities to learn.

The good news is also that we have the brilliant truth tellers and powerful educators to illuminate the darkness. The good news is that we have located some of the missing voices, and they have spoken eloquently. The good news is that there are many more to locate. As one of the authors has said, the question is, "Will there be listeners?" Success is within our grasp at any moment that we choose to reach for it. The only question is will we reach for it.

I am truly grateful to Lisa Delpit who brought all of us together, to the wonderful colleagues that she chose, and to the editors, Dowdy and Wynne, for collecting our stories. No more silenced dialogue, no more other people's children, no more missing voices.

References

Adler, Eric (2003). "Principal at KC's African-themed elementary school knows how to reach kids—and parents, too." *Kansas City Star* (Kansascity.com) September 28.

Berliner, David and Biddle, Bruce J. (1995). *The manufactured Crisis: Myths, fraud, and the attack on America's public schools.* Cambridge: Perseus Books.

Comer, J. P. (1980). *School power.* New York Free Press.

Cubberly, E. P. (1920). *The history of education.* New York: Houghton Mifflin.

Delpit, L. (1995). *Other people's children: Cultural conflict in the classroom.* New York: The New Press.

Edwards, L. (1996) *The power of ideas: The Heritage Foundation at 25 Years:* Jameson Books.

Harrison, L. E. and Huntington, S. P. (Eds.) (2000). *Culture matters: How values shape human progress.* New York: Basic Books.

Herrenstein, Richard and Murray, Charles (1994) *The bell curve: Intelligence and class structure in American life.* New York: The Free Press.

Hilliard, Asa G. III (1984). "Democratizing the common school in a multicultural society." *Education and Urban Society.* 16, 3, 262–273.

Hugar, T. (2003). Unpublished memo.

Jensen, Arthur (1980). *Bias in mental testing.* New York: Free Press.

Lynn, R. and Vanhanen, T. (2002). *IQ and the Wealth of Nations.* Westport, CT: Praeger.

Smith, D. (2003). "KC principal sues school district." *The Kansas City Star,* September 27.

Thernstrom, A. and Thernstrom, S. (2003). *No excuses: Closing the racial gap in learning.* New York: Simon and Schuster.

Chapter 1

Interview with Lisa Delpit

When you were in the planning stage of the Urban Atlanta Coalition Compact, what was your biggest expectation of this project to effect school change?

Through the co-reform effort, I expected that everyone associated with the project would fully understand that poor children of color in urban schools can excel, not just meet minimum standards. I also expected that principals would take on the challenge of reform as their own, that they would keep moving on issues even after the funded program was over.

I'll get back to those expectations later, but for now, let's focus on what you discovered about teachers during the project. While working with the seven schools, what were some of the major challenges that you observed teachers face?

One of the biggest challenges for them seemed to be changing their own negative belief systems about children and families that they served. Many of them were convinced, at least when we first met with them, that their students who lived in poverty, especially poor Black children, could not read or write well or do math well because of the perceived "deficits" of their parents. This attitude created other challenges for these teachers. It kept them from taking responsibility for their instruction. They tended to blame the children and their parents for failing test scores instead of examining those failures as possibly a result of faulty classroom instructional practices.

In addition, some teachers would get bogged down in blaming their failures on the central office. They would seem to get stuck there, feeling powerless to change classroom practices or academic achievement levels because the system, they believed, often did not offer appropriate support or resources for their work.

I think that their learning to work together for change, to view the school as a whole, not just individual classrooms, was a tremendous leap that some teachers made;

and others did not. Those who did learn to struggle with a collaborative process were exciting to be around. Their enthusiasm for the children, for change, for their own professional growth became contagious at some schools. Yet at others, teachers who did not participate in the collaborative process became threatened by or jealous of what the effective teachers were accomplishing in their classrooms.

Another obstacle to their success as teachers was their failure to learn how to relate to and communicate with parents. Too few of the teachers came to us knowing how to see parents as partners, not as obstacles to overcome.

There seemed to be little effort made to learning about the kids and their communities. Helping teachers see the parents' and children's strengths where they previously only saw pathologies and problems posed a serious challenge. In the application process, we rarely heard administrators or teachers talk about the positive power of the children; of what the parents brought to the table; or of the good things going on in the communities. They didn't know or understand the valuable contributions that the Black churches were making in the communities or what some of the single mothers were doing to protect the physical well-being of the children in their neighborhoods. Instead, what we consistently heard from people in schools in the beginning was that these parents did not "value education" and "did not help the children with their homework." What the students did not know or did not do, their weaknesses, seemed the total focus of the beginning conversations about poor children in schools.

I think maybe another challenge I saw was just instruction that was total lecture, very little student engagement, a lot of time spent on discipline, with some of the teachers, not all of them. And often just not a very child-friendly setting existed. Sometimes, in those classrooms, I was falling asleep, I know the kids were.

To be fair, I wasn't shocked by the attitudes because seldom do teacher education programs give any attention to helping teachers learn about students or families or communities. Typically the focus is solely on content and technique. No wonder these teachers, who usually enter the profession with the best of intentions, are often left resenting their students and the students' families because they have no tools with which to deepen their understanding of the children's communities and cultural knowledge or to develop collaborative relationships with parents. I know that many of these basically wonderful people could change their perspectives, once they had the opportunity to develop new insights and strategies to achieve their instructional goals.

What main challenges do you think the parents faced in those communities in relationship to their schools?

The challenges varied, depending on the school. One of the schools we worked with was predominantly European American and middle class, and in that school some African American parents probably had a hard time feeling comfortable enough to come in. Maya [my daughter] had gone to a school similar to this one, and while Maya attended there, I interviewed some of the other Black parents. They said that they felt so unwelcome in the school that they decided that there wasn't any point in coming there. I think that held true for parents at some of the other schools. The attitudes that the school held about parents and some of the attitudes that other parents held about parents were reform challenges. It was interesting that in the all-Black schools, many times the parents who did come into the schools to participate, and could for whatever reasons, were harder on parents who didn't even though sometimes those parents who didn't come to school had very good reasons for not coming: multiple jobs, sick children, having to ride a bus, not having cars, or just exhaustion.

The short answer is that the people who participated in the schools in general, parents, teachers, principals, had very negative views of those who participated less. That was the major thing. I am not sure how the parents could feel that they were really getting a good sense of what their kids were learning. I am not sure if they did or not. I know one of the stresses for the teachers was the mandated tests. The teachers and principals were under a great deal of stress that they were going to lose their jobs and all manner of things were going to happen if test scores didn't go up. That caused a lot of frenzied energy that was not connected to really educating children, and that dilemma still continues.

That seems to be a pervasive problem across the country, certainly not just with UACC schools, but what do you see as an antidote to that?
I don't know. I am struggling with that . . . I can say that for the most part, the schools that have created excellent results for children who you wouldn't expect to do well on those standardized tests have not focused on the tests for the most part. They have focused on developing the teaching. But I'm not sure exactly what they do, and I don't know that I know enough yet to be able to feel comfortable saying to a school, "Just ignore the tests and this is what you do." I think we haven't looked enough at what is done in those effective schools. It is not one thing, it is a whole bevy of very intricately connected pieces that involve instruction, the school building, relationships to parents, relationships to the outside community, relationships between teachers, just a lot of things. I don't know that there is a prescription that we can say yet . . . do all of these things and the kids will have high test scores. I think Asa [Hilliard] said that the key is creating opportunities for teachers and others to collaborate, and I believe it to be the case. That is the reason we set up UACC the way we did. But collaboration requires some leadership in learning what to collaborate about. If the collaboration is only around the question of "How do you raise the test scores?" vs. "How do we best educate these young children in our charge?" then I don't think anyone will be successful. Teachers, instead, will start looking at, "Which program do we get? This program or that program? Or can we figure out a time after school where our students can do more of these drills on the test?" For significant instructional change, there has to be some leadership (usually from the principal, I think) that gets people to think beyond just the immediate goal of raising test scores. Teachers, principals, parents need to collaborate by

all thinking more deeply about how to educate our children, how to develop them as critical thinkers before the long term goal of raising test scores will happen.

That makes me think of another question when you mentioned the leadership, what was your experience in UACC schools with issues that might be particular to only principals or leadership? I know you had a component in the UACC that involved working with principals as a separate entity.

We tried to meet with principals in a more relaxed setting, over dinner, at home; had Betty Strickland [former interim superintendent of Atlanta Public School System] come to talk with them; yet, that wasn't enough.

What did you see as their particular struggles, and how important is leadership with school reform?

I think it is clear. It is very vital in any setting, even at the university. The climate of the place is often determined by its leadership. We [university professors] feel that way based on the leadership of the dean at a university, and teachers feel that based on the principal. I think their struggles, again . . . most of them started and were pushed to start with the idea of "How do we raise the test scores?" as the primary issue. When you start with that, then it seems like, "Oh, we raised test scores by doing more and more and more and more of test practice and test review." And sometimes less than ethical practices in terms of testing happen because we make the stakes so high.

In some settings the principals were told very strongly that they might be out of a job if test scores didn't go up. When you do that, people are going to do what they can in the short term to make test scores go up. I think because of that, several of the principals were less tolerant with creative teachers than they should have been. And they ended up losing a lot of their really good teachers. Of course, we know of a couple of instances of that because the teachers chafed against the idea of just doing rote test review constantly or having kids sit quietly and memorize things. The teachers wanted engagement, and a lot of times the principals were afraid of that because it wasn't focused on the test scores.

Another challenge for a couple of principals was that they had difficulty figuring out how to get rid of teachers who weren't performing well. They felt, in the instance I am thinking about, that you should support people and support teachers, which is a good thing, but sometimes they would do it for too long . . . when teachers did too much damage to kids and didn't teach them.

Also, a couple of principals were having a lot of personal issues at the same time. This, of course, affects people's work. Principals did not seem to have adequate support systems, which might allow for someone else in the school to take up some of the slack. In part, because the school had been set up as such a hierarchy, the principal was the person on top, and everybody else was below. I think if these schools had been set up in a more collaborative way, then, when any individual was struggling with personal issues, others at the school could have taken the lead.

One particular system where many of our teachers worked was very hierarchical, and there wasn't a power base for teachers at all. This was a school system that had no bargaining, which meant that teachers literally had no power. So there was no sense that teachers could take on leadership. We were trying to push teacher leadership in schools, but we were being fought against by the system in essence and the culture of the system. Not individuals but the whole culture of the system was antithetical to that notion of collaboration and of non-hierarchy.

Creating a culture of collaboration takes, I believe, a long-term commitment to a school, while at the same time having some authority in the larger system. You can't force collaboration on a principal who doesn't want it unless there is some impetus to push him or her in that direction. The principal has to buy into the collaborative process or it withers on the vine. When teachers develop new ideas together and they're ignored, and when all decisions are made from the top with no discussion, collaborative efforts are undermined. Any project seeking to develop collaboration in a school had better insure a cooperative principal at the outset at best, or a central office supervisor who can "encourage" the principal to move in the desired direction at worst.

Once a principal is on board it takes a consistent presence in a school to break down the barriers of individualism. Unfortunately we didn't have the personnel to provide this. If we had, I would have liked to create small problem-solving teams, such as a team to explore how to increase literacy learning in the lunchroom, or how to establish an area devoted to making parents feel comfortable to visit the school. People new to cooperative decision-making often need consistent assistance early on.

This is a bit of a shift in our discussion, but what was your experience in trying to pull together five colleges and universities to collaborate on this particular effort?

I don't know if it's a weakness or strength of mine, but I chose not to go to the leadership in those colleges but to the people who we thought could do the work, the faculty members who could do the work. Thus, we got people who wanted to do the work. However, we didn't necessarily get support from their institutions for the work they were doing. That was a really big challenge. I know if we had gone just to the leadership, then the focus would have become "What can we as an institution get out of this collaboration?" which would have changed who they might have assigned to it and what they wanted from it. We, on the other hand, were really anxious to have people who were invested in changing the schools for African American kids.

It wasn't easy because I found we had to try to give a lot of support to those faculties, many of whom were young faculty. Many had to leave the project because they couldn't continue to work at the tenure process and get the kinds of things that they needed for their careers from the work that we were trying to do. Many of them did persevere, in spite of that, which is certainly to their credit. But in some ways it wasn't officially, even though it was technically, a collaboration of universities; it really was a collaboration of individuals who were stationed at different universities. But that was the case with us, too, because I wouldn't say that our university was behind what we did. It was the individuals at the university who were committed to the work.

Because this component of the project, university fellows, was such a vital part of UACC, and a part needed to connect the reform effort to university education programs, I would do it the same way again were we to replicate the project. However, I would find more money to allow more "buy-out" time (or fewer schools to serve) and more time to meet together to identify potential research possibilities.

There are a number of different components to the program, such as teacher leadership, parent involvement, community involvement, development of a cadre of university fellow liaisons that you just addressed. Which one of the many facets of the program did you find the most effective?

I think it was when we could get in there and work with teachers. When we could get the space and time for teachers to communicate with each other; for example, the retreats for teachers where they began to get a sense of who the other participants were and where they began to develop a collective commitment. That had the potential for the most change. The problem was that we just did not have enough staff and funding to continue to do that as much as it was needed. I, of course, initially wanted to work with two schools, but we were pushed by the funding source to expand; and they wanted it to be more than seven. There just were not enough resources to do as much of that kind of teacher development work. If we could have done that more; if we could have had a continued period of time with groups of teachers; if we could have had fellows in the school for protracted periods of time, directing meetings, working to help people collaborate, to help people come to agreements, broader success, I think, would have happened.

It was certainly really exciting, too, when the different school communities met together. We facilitated a number of those meetings. The schools seemed to really like that. The teachers liked the opportunity to talk to teachers from other schools which, of course, is something else that almost never happens, opportunities for discussing some of the same issues that they all faced. Those kinds of things probably create the best possibilities for change, and, maybe, working with the principals at the same time as teachers has the potential for getting the greatest change. Again the lack of adequate resources, especially human resources, prevented the project from being executed the way it should have been executed.

Were there any other specific challenges in any of those components that you would like to address, that you haven't already addressed, specifically teacher leadership being a problem with the system and how to empower teachers?

It isn't just not knowing how to empower teachers; it's often not wanting to. Systems are often set up that teachers have no power. And that, of course, presents a problem because then if something doesn't work in the classroom that has been mandated from the top, the teachers feel absolved from any responsibility for it. Thus it not only takes the power, it takes all of the responsibility from the people who are really in the setting, in the classroom. That is a terrible model because then you just don't try. If you feel that it is not your responsibility, if it is not . . . you say, "Oh, well they said to do it, that's why I am doing it." Therefore, for a professional, "top-down" leadership makes teaching a very non-engaging and a mind-numbing situation.

There was the parent involvement, an issue which I think you covered well and then the community involvement and the attitude about how to do that.

And I am sure they didn't have the resources either, to really develop parental leadership and engagement. We certainly tried. We set up the Urban Teacher Leadership Master's Degree Program to try to help teachers understand how they could get resources from other arenas and make contacts with community resources, but that is typically not done, and teachers are not taught how to think about connecting to the communities. If they do it, it is one teacher doing it on his or her own. That is unfortunate, because teaching really is a broader . . . to do it effectively, it takes a village to teach a child, and to do it effectively teachers have TO be a part of all of that.

At one point you talked about teachers within the Urban Teacher Leadership Master's Program, actually either taking classes or connecting with community organizers or learning from labor organizers how to organize. Would you in retrospect, put that as maybe a component of a similar UACC effort of school reform?

I think I would not say that everybody should do it. It would have to be people who would see themselves that way . . . because teaching is exhausting. There are those who have the energy and excitement about doing the kind of organizing work that community organizers might do and incorporating that into their teaching. Everybody could be exposed to it, but I think people would need to self-select in terms of thinking about how involved they want to become in that kind of movement. I think a lot of them would, actually, given the opportunity. A lot of the teachers really felt for the first time that they had some leadership potential, that they could shine outside of the classroom. That was really empowering, I think, for the teachers as well as for the kids that they were teaching.

Organizing for teachers and schools could take a number of different forms. Schools and/or teachers might organize a number of significant constituents:

- retired teachers to help in schools;
- parent involvement
- community/church groups
- grandparents
- community centers to connect after school programs with school goals

We were fortunate in our city that we had leaders like Dr. Alonzo A. Crim and Dr. Betty Strickland, both former superintendents, who had, actually, years ago led the way administratively in organizing community people, parents, and churches to assist schools in reaching their academic goals. What we needed to do was to help teachers begin to learn those organizing skills.

What outcomes of the program are you particularly pleased about?

In some ways, I don't know what a lot of the outcomes are because I think a lot of them are continuing. I think that one important result was planting the seeds in some teachers that they could become change agents in their classrooms, their schools and their city, and their school system. I think we were beginning to see many teachers in each system do that, and that will develop even further. Just having a different mind set for a few folks made reform efforts begin taking a momentum of their own. I know that was the case for some parents, too, whom Folami was able to nurture and put into positions of leadership, who really became very active in what they were doing. I am sure nothing will stop those parents now.

The Action Teams at each school as well as the leadership workshops that the project sponsored, I think, were quite effective in helping teachers and parents begin to believe in their own leadership capacity and their ability to influence professional decisions in and out of schools.

In addition, I think that the university fellows came away with a new understanding of the challenges that were going on in the schools, and it affected and will continue to affect their teaching in their university classrooms. All of them actually did say that they felt that they were teaching differently as a result of having been involved in the schools. That was a good thing, too. The more we can get pre-service and graduate-level teachers to understand some of the realities that are going on in schools, the better connected our universities will be to the schools.

What would you say were some of the biggest surprises for you in the program?

How difficult it was for people to work together. I had not realized how difficult it would be in the schools for folk to be able to work collaboratively, what kind of obstacles would have to be overcome to get them to do that. . . . That is the biggest thing. It was almost easier to change people's attitudes about children than it was to change the attitudes about working together.

I think that was one of Folami's surprises, too, how faculty did not work together, and she assumed that some of the UACC teacher leaders would be able to go back into the school and get more to happen amongst the other faculty.

If you were to begin again as the PI, what might you change in the program?

I would work with fewer schools or more money. We really had great ideas, but we just didn't have the resources to carry them out. For instance, as I mentioned before, the university fellows piece of the project was important. Our retreats, where we gathered faculty, parents, administrators together to bond and to discuss goals and challenges of the project met with great success—but we needed more funding to host those retreats more often as we were struggling through difficult issues. Our Urban Expos were phenomenal successes, but, again, we needed more support for those in order to bring more constituents to those events and trainings. Our "town hall" meetings, where we brought Action Teams, Parent Teams, administrators, etc. together from all the schools to discuss the successes and challenges of the reform effort also were effective. I would incorporate more of those into future efforts.

In an earlier conversation, you started saying that it takes time to change a school and that it is often easier to start a school.
A change of culture is not an easy process. And there was not enough time because we had to keep adding schools; we didn't have enough time, because we worked within the changing culture. People forget that. The two schools where Comer worked took fourteen years to change; yet everybody wants this quick fix. And if reform doesn't work in one year, then, we most often change it and get something else. So there is no opportunity to really develop the kinds of things that we need to develop, the relationships, changes in the ways people look at each other, other teachers, parents, kids. That is all really important to people. You can't rush it. Rather than more prescriptiveness, if you think about it over time, making definite parameters for the change might be appropriate initially, but you should back off more and more of that as you develop people's ability to collaborate and think together. But you need someone there regularly working to help people do that.

The other significant factor was that UACC had no authority. Charles Payne has said that people are not necessarily going to change because we think it is a good idea that they change, because it is hard work. If they don't have any outside pressure saying, "You have to do this or look at that," they are less likely to think it is important. Not having any official connection with the school system and not having enough time were two significant obstacles to the work of reform. I guess it is like teaching where you first have to establish a sort of rapport and climate. You have to give people the rules of how to work together and the rules of what will be allowed and won't be allowed. And once you do that, then you begin to give them and the kids more responsibility and authority to take on tasks. That is probably what you have to do in school systems too. Maybe that is where my prescriptiveness was coming from. I don't think it is the end-all, be-all, but it may be a place where you have to start so you can get people to the place where they can then get so excited about what they are doing that change is worthwhile and desired.

Let me ask you one other thing. You mentioned that in Comer's school reform, for some schools it took 14 years for significant change, and many of us assume that

education is an organic process that happens over time. I have heard Asa Hilliard say that schools can change the academic achievement level of children in a year. So how do we compute both of those because both are true?

The case with us and with Comer is that we were both outside entities coming into the school or system, and the schools that Asa is talking about were more "inside" the leadership. The leadership within the schools was already on board for change or reform. We, however, were in a position where we had to try pushing the leadership to change as well as the teachers. That made a difference.

In our application process, we required all schools who wanted to participate to submit a commitment document where 80 percent of their faculty signed, agreeing to accept and to implement the UACC reform effort at their school. Unfortunately, what we found after the first year was that many of the faculty signed without understanding what it was they were signing up for.

Chapter 2
Joan T. Wynne & F. Prescott-Adams

Interview with Folami Prescott-Adams, Director of the UACC

Folami, as you went through the reform process with the UACC project, what did you learn about the role of an African American woman as a leader in school reform?

It's difficult to separate the "woman thing" from the African American leadership role, but I'll try. I felt that being an African American in the schools was helpful. We have, particularly in the city's public schools, had a number of African Americans at the top level of leadership for many years at the superintendent level. As far back as I can remember, we've had African American superintendents. So I didn't think in any way it was a disadvantage. Particularly, at the teacher and the parent level, it was an advantage because I was an African American who lived in the city. My children went to the public schools. The school people saw me as someone who had the same concerns, who was taking the same risks as they were in terms of entrusting the city's public schools with my children. So again, I felt that it was an advantage in that way.

But I need to respond to that question also as it relates to the other two systems involved in the project. In those, my being a Black woman was different, had a different impact. I felt that in many cases, it was a disadvantage. In one of those systems, as you know, we have these issues of north area White and wealthy, south area Black and middle-to-low income. And it is so thick and complex. I have to be careful what I say here, but I think there is some subtle racism that exists in a system, in a district like that where people begin to ask, "Why is it those poor black children can't do as well as those kids in the north part of the district?" Then, I become just a part of the problem because

I look like the south part of the district, as weird as that sounds. One of the other systems of the three that the compact served was a more progressive district, but leadership has been White for a long time and, particularly, the Board of Education.

There, as well as in the other district with the south vs. north dichotomy, the schools felt challenged dealing with anyone who said we need to talk about race. They just didn't want to talk about it. They wanted to believe that the whole color-blind notion is the solution, and, they would say, "We just need to help all of our kids." When I think of the problems we had, especially, at School W, I would almost guarantee that if there were a team of Whites leading UACC that maintained what we said, "We have to look at the small number of African Americans at the school who are continuously left back, who do not come to school with the same skills as your middle-class students," it would have been perceived in a different way because the person saying it was White. I think there would have still been resistance, don't get me wrong, but I think it would have been a different level of resistance, almost like the whole good ole' boy network: "Let's close the door and talk about this. You are right, we shouldn't be having 11 students who are left back and who are all black boys. You're right, but let's close the door and talk about this, girlfriend." The good ole boy network that we did not have. I think that my leadership as a Black woman in this system also led to more defensiveness from the White teachers.

Back in the schools, in the raising-money issue, I think Black leadership was a problem in a lot of ways. Atlanta's corporate community and philanthropic community seemed to appreciate a rainbow coalition. If we had a team that was meeting with people from the Coca-Cola Foundation or whatever foundation, it doesn't matter which one, if our team had consisted of a White male, I think that they would have received us in a different way. (We had a White female, but often because she had such similar philosophies to the Black leadership, I think she was almost seen as the honorary White who really thinks like those Black people.)

Again, I hate to say this, but if our leadership had included a White male, it would have allowed us to raise money more easily than we did. In addition, because Lisa Delpit is so strong in her convictions, unwilling to surrender to the donors her experienced approach to reform, and said this loudly and clearly, some people did not want to give money to people like Lisa who are not going to let them at least think that they are running things. Because people do play those games. They say, "Well, we want to hear from our funders on what you think are the solutions." And the funder might say, "I think you need to give those poor kids a library for their home." Some people actually play the game and say, "OK," and still do what they want to do but also give books to kids. And I don't think Lisa would have ever done that. She would have made it clear that wasn't the solution. I think that attitude scared funders.

What about your major funder? Did you sense that your ethnicity had any play in that?

I didn't think so when I started, when I was dealing on the telephone and all of that. However, when I went to the national meeting and saw that I was the only African American director (there was one other woman in New York, but she left and went to Scholastic) that scared me. Now remember that most of these projects served urban areas, yet the people in charge were White.

How many projects were funded by the major foundation?

About 12 projects. That means 11 White directors; there were some lower-level staff people in that group. There may have been two African Americans if you include the staff people.

How many of those were women?

About half. To me they also seemed more corporate. I can't really speak to everybody's background, but I do know that everyone did not come from an educational arena. The local directors of the other Annenberg Challenge sites seemed more concerned about the importance of writing a good report and coalition building at a kind of Chamber of Commerce level. They seemed to believe it was important to spend a lot of their time holding events that may empower parents or engage teachers, but their main purpose seemed to be to bring the mayor and the mayor's associates for education and the corporate giving community to their events. Some of us laughed at the amount of money that was spent on glossy reports. That approach reminds me very much of a corporate environment. So again in that room where I was not just the only African American director, once we lost the other woman, but one of the youngest, I often felt ignored. My eclectic background (my private school experience, my experience running a federally funded drug prevention program and directing the educational program for the 100 Black Men of Atlanta, Inc.), I thought, gave me such a unique opportunity to bring all of those experiences together in a school reform setting. I was excited about what I had to bring to the table, but in that setting, again, I felt sometimes that the others in the room were thinking, "Why is she here and why did she get this job?"

I also think that some of those people wanted to see Lisa Delpit there. Where's Lisa? How's Lisa? We know, and maybe even some of them knew, that the primary reason our university was able to get this grant was because of Lisa Delpit and the work she has done and the respect the Foundation had for her work. I think we all knew that she could articulate what she said in her book in a way that could have some positive impact on children in disenfranchised communities. So I think that, too, was big for them. I felt as though they were saying, "I want Lisa here, we want Lisa's brain." So I would often feel like the (I'm careful to say this because I have step children) step child. "She's young; she's black; she's not Lisa."

Nevertheless, we did have a few directors that had been principals, well actually, we had one that was a principal; and she got a lot of attention for having been a principal and for being a director. I want to say that was Utah. She was a dynamo as well.

Once I spoke in meetings, people often would come up to me afterwards and say things like "I think you're brilliant" or something like that because they wanted to connect with me. But I did wonder how Annenberg saw me. I don't know. They seemed more concerned about money issues than teacher/student issues. I often felt as though they were thinking, "Just go see how they're spending our money." I don't know if you remember this, Joannie, but Walter Annenberg did not like his staff to travel. He wanted them to stay in Pennsylvania, and so that's why often they weren't at the meetings. If the meetings were in other cities, the staff often were not there.

What would you say were your biggest obstacles in working with the foundations?
I really hate to say this but I have to, their own unawareness of the challenges. They did not really understand all of the dynamics of schools. I won't even say of school reform. I will say of schools. Here's an example: I mentioned that a funder might give books to kids, and that really did happen. To me this is a perfect example of funders who don't really have a clue, who want to see change in five years. You cannot change a system that took clearly 100 years to construct. The public school system in this country has been in existence for 100 years at least. You can't just change it in five years. And this notion that Lisa had of professional capacity-building, of building competence, of spending money on skills, on things that you can't see, but when the money dries up those intangibles are still there in your building, your school. I think that was very hard for them and buying books for kids were easy to see. Glossy reports. That was easy. I think the evaluation piece was all over the place. There was very little leadership from Annenberg in a holistic way, "This is what we need to document in terms of pre-data, process data, formative data and summative data." And I don't think they had a clue. I didn't see them meeting with people who have a reputation of doing evaluation in school reform projects to get that. So I sometimes worried that the motives weren't clear.

I remember the story that was told about Walter Annenberg and Ann Gregory, sitting over dinner and asking "What can we do about urban and rural schools." Ambassador Annenberg responds saying, "I've got half a billion dollars to contribute toward solving the problem." I think that was a tremendous challenge that you have the money and the good intention, but you don't have the expertise. In those circumstances it seems that you would have to be willing to let go of some of your control of how the money is spent and who gets it.

For instance, one of the stipulations they had was that the school systems couldn't get the money directly. I don't think that was a bad idea. I think that was actually good because, otherwise, the money also would have just gotten sucked into, you know, some additional computers and huge budgets. But I look at the match problem that we had and that I'm sure some of the other sites had as well, and again you ask yourself,

"How deeply did they think about how that would really work?" I know the idea was let's get the local community to buy in, but maybe the mass commitment could have been after five years instead of after the first year.

It might have been more effective to allow five years to demonstrate how to build a foundation, then, maybe to get the local giving community to begin buying in year two and three and have a role at an advisory board level. At the least a system or local foundation might incorporate some of their human resources that they have already provided to schools or communities into the work of the project, and possibly they could commit to giving money after the five years. I don't think, though, that Annenberg was open to hearing these suggestions for matching money. They never created a forum for that.

So I think raising the local dollars is a tremendous challenge, and it's probably the reason Lisa took such a hard stand here locally on not allowing the local giving community to tell us how we do the work we need to do. But I think as educators, Joannie, we also have to learn how to tell our stories and to help people understand the complexities. I think Lisa's book is a good example of how someone can do that because I've seen many White educators, in particular, "get" that book even though it hurts for them to say, "It's a hard read, but I got it."

What would you say were some of the most difficult pieces in directing the project locally?

Well, it's somewhat about this notion of "capacity building." I think it took a good year, maybe a year and a half, to really build a vision that teachers, parents, administrators, and teacher educators could all grasp. But then, again, I don't know if we ever really built a clear vision of the role of the teacher educator. I think we tried some things, and I think some of the fellows established some really good relationships with their schools, but I don't think we ever figured out how to take those lessons we learned and incorporate them into a teacher education curriculum at the various universities that participated. Influencing teacher education programs was one of our original goals.

But imagine a school system that spends $30,000 at the drop of a hat, and we're offering them only $30,000 a year. They didn't understand that for a minute. I'm sure they thought, "Why is $30,000 a big deal? Why are we trying hard for this money?" The initial application plans were very basic: those proposals where the schools initially created a plan of how they were to spend the money and what some of their strengths were.

Their plans were too basic? Is that what you mean?

Yes, I don't think they spent enough time thinking of what kind of competency the teachers actually needed. And when I say vision, I also mean that we had to build a belief system that we could truly make a difference for our kids, where they could effectively learn, where their parents could be actively engaged in their schools. We spent a lot of time redefining parent roles. I think we realized that when teachers said, "I need my parents to be involved," they really meant that they wanted the parents to sign the report card, come to the parent-teacher conference, and look at the child's homework. But many of them didn't really want an empowered parent.

When I now tell people that lesson I learned, a lot of educators say to me, "Well, look when you say empowerment, I hope you don't mean you think parents should be in here telling teachers what to do." I say, "No, I didn't say that." But if a parent doesn't know they have a right to be at the table when the I.E.P. (Individualized Education Plan) is being developed, if they have a problem with some of what the plan states, then, the parents need to know that they have the right to be informed. They need to understand what an I.E.P. is; what special needs are; and how schools are meeting their children's special needs. And how often is their child ostracized? When they, as parents, should be more active or, at least, vocal?

So you are saying, then, that this was probably one of the most difficult pieces for you as a director?

Yes, building a vision that they could all share as well as an awareness that you could have a school reform movement that wasn't funded by millions of dollars. That was the philosophy, I believe, that we had, that it really wasn't about money because the money is already there. We might need to redirect funds, which we tried to do, and that was one of the goals. I don't think we were able to redirect as much as we would have liked.

If you had served fewer schools (you served seven at the beginning), if you had worked with half as many, three, maybe, four schools instead of seven, do you think that would have created a better opportunity to build a vision faster?

I do. When we had seven schools, we had seven personalities. Seven school personalities. Very different dynamics in every building, a different principal in every building. Different levels of buy-in from principals from the district. And so, yes, I think that was a challenge. Although, I think having been a multi-district project was, at the same time, a plus. It allowed, first of all, teachers to realize how similar some of the challenges [across the districts] were. Number two, it allowed for getting them to move beyond the particulars of the dynamics within their individual districts. When it was all teachers from one system together in the room, people might moan about "how the district keeps changing this or that, or how "they" [the system administrators] don't know what "they" are doing, or how we have a whole new board, and they don't know education." But with three different systems represented in the same room, we did not have to confront that kind of complaining, and that was helpful.

Also we learned that a lot of students do move among those three districts. So teachers and administrators realized they really were serving very similar communities. But at times, yes, I think you are right that if we had served a smaller number of schools, we could have had more impact. But, you know, what we really needed? We needed a change agent who became that insider/outsider. We thought the university fellows did that. But this was just one thing on their very full plates.

What do you mean by insider/outsider?

Someone from outside the day-to-day school community but who knew the school well enough to be an insider, who knew the teachers, and the teachers knew her, someone who knew some of the dynamics of the schools, who might even know the budget at some level. For example at one of the schools, we began near the end to pay attention to Title I funding and some opportunities to redirect Title one funding in a more appropriate way to meet other needs of the school. We didn't have anybody who could spend enough time in the school building, to be that kind of insider/outsider. Visits once or at best twice a week were not enough to adequately build the relationships needed with parents, teachers, students, nor was it enough time to get a handle on the overall dynamics of each school.

Do you think if you had "bought out" more of each fellow's time from the university, maybe two classes instead of one, university fellows might have made a more significant impact?

I definitely think that would have helped. Now we do have another dynamic around the notion of the university professor being somebody who is here to get my research, and I remember we had one principal in particular who just believed we were in the building to get research that was going to help us and not help her school. So that's one challenge. I'm saying "yes" if we had more of the time of the fellow and possibly even the fellow's input in the development of the project conceptually. I think that would have helped. But we would have always had the challenge of convincing public school educators that university faculty really care about the schools they were serving and not just the fellows' own research and tenure.

How about the teachers? When you worked with teachers in the school, what seemed to be their biggest frustrations about reform efforts?

I think a lot of teachers misunderstood what reform was, and they thought if the school adopted a reading program, that was reform. It is not. And in their defense, they've seen so many reform efforts come and go that many of them started off with the attitude, "Oh, here's another one, and it'll be gone so why should I get into it because whatever they say we can't do it." They seemed to have so little confidence about what the students could do and what they as teachers had the power to do to change the children's performance. Often the teachers would say that they wanted to hear from us, but they didn't really.

Nevertheless, we began to convince them to try change. I think partly because we put teachers in leadership positions, often with the principal out of the room. We paid them for their time, which is a most direct way of saying we respect you; we respect your expertise. We also fed them. Seems small, doesn't it, but feeding people healthy meals for their evening events made a difference to them.

Yes, and I know that your insistence on doing that was because of its cultural relevance. You knew that part of the African tradition as well as the southern culture is building relationship by breaking bread together.

Yes. Another important thing that we did for teachers was bringing in other educators from across the country to enter into real dialogue with them, not just as talking heads. I'll talk about the Expo more in a bit, but that was phenomenal to them to again not just have a conference where you have a speaker and then you go to sessions and you're told "O.K. this year we are going to do 'Success for all' and this is the 'So & So' consultant and you'll have seven days of training, and here are the text books."

Rather we were saying "Look at some different models and which ones really work for you? Which of these people do you think could really be helpful to your school?" I saw one school's faculty get so excited about Professor B's math program, so excited, and, then, hit those walls where the district says "That's not how we teach math." So again they began to feel as though it was all "hot air," that you're saying reform, but can you really back it up? They thought, "You say you want to hear from the teacher, and you want the teachers to make decisions about the types of reform and training support and other types of resource support that they need, but are you really going to be able to back it up when someone at the central office says "Professor B doesn't use a text book." I don't think so.

Let me ask you about teachers and collaboration because a lot of your work was built on collaboration with multiple levels and multiple partners. Let's focus on just the teachers. What were the challenges in building collaborations amongst teachers? We all know the sense of isolation that teachers often feel. What did you see worked with them? What were some of those challenges in helping them build collaborative bodies amongst themselves?

Let me talk about collaborations within the school building first. There's a sad dynamic that happens in schools, and this may happen in other settings. And that is the consequence of when you shine, when you're very good, when your students learn and engage, and when they want you back the next year; and the teachers and parents petition for you; and your students still stay with you year after year. When all of these good things happen, instead of people coming to you for ideas, you're isolated even more. So we had to fight that culture. Because we were saying "that teacher is your friend and we do want to highlight his/her work because it's working, and there are some things that you could learn from that person."

I don't know how these attitudes evolve. I don't know if this is a human nature thing or what, but people seemed to think that we were saying that "You're the problem, be like her." Kind of like the parent who says "I wish you'd be more like Joannie." And that's how they hear it, and we don't mean that. We were just trying to highlight effective practices, and to suggest that we could all learn from those practices. Antoine Fisher's autobiography mentions a teacher who changed his life, and I found myself folding back those pages wanting to share with other teachers. Yet even as I was folding the pages, I knew many of the teachers would want to deflect that particular teachers' successes by saying, "I'm not like that, she had a loving husband; she didn't have any kids at home, etc. etc."

So you saw a lot of that attitude?
Always. At least one person in a school would either say it directly to me or say it to another teacher who would share it with me. Many people don't like you pointing out a successful teacher. We called them most effective. The other teachers didn't like that, and the teacher who is highlighted often doesn't like it because it seemed to bring another level of isolation. Some of the teachers tried to say that there were other reasons a teacher was so effective, something that's irrelevant, like "She doesn't have kids at home; or she is a new teacher; or she doesn't have the issues I have." So excuses and isolation were definitely challenges.

Another serious issue blocking collaborative efforts among teachers was that a teacher was often afraid to give up her classroom to a substitute in order to go visit another teacher's classroom so that she could learn from others. We tried to do collaborations within the school day where a teacher could observe another teacher, or she could co-teach a class or co-plan. That meant, however, that someone else had to teach her class, and it's really interesting how the average teacher says her kids fall behind with substitutes. Perhaps we could look at school systems hiring a substitute teacher who's assigned to one school or one or two schools. There's always going to be somebody absent, right? Any given day in one or two schools, and then that substitute is on the staff; knows the kids; knows the curriculum. Then, maybe teachers wouldn't believe their students would fall behind just because a substitute is in their classrooms.

So you're saying that there seemed to be a prevalence of professional jealousy against effective teachers and that some teachers didn't want to give over their classrooms to a substitute. Did you notice any other issues concerning teachers and collaboration?
Yes, we were attempting to engage people in transformation and not just training, transformation of core beliefs about pedagogy, school based decision-making processes, meaningful parental engagement, and perceptions of family life. They needed to collaborate around those issues and not just be content to write up a plan or budget. A lot of teachers just haven't had a chance to build their own skills as leaders of a collaborative effort. I'm talking now about basic things like facilitating meetings, making sure every voice is heard, and understanding that one vocal person should not be doing most of the talking. They needed to learn that there are some people who have incredible ideas, but they're shy; and if you don't facilitate the gathering of the group well, then you never get to hear from them.

Did many of the teachers you served lack those kinds of skills?
Yes, and finding ways to energize people if a meeting is at the end of the day.

And as I remember, you did offer sessions where you brought teachers together to help train them in those kinds of skills.
Yes, and we did have some teachers who really became extremely good at it.

Did you create those seminars as a result of noticing that teachers did not have these skills and as a consequence were not collaborating well?
These happened because we had created a chair, the action team leader. Therefore, in each school there were six to ten people who were leading this reform effort, and they were called the action team. They were the ones who would write the actual plan after getting input from others. They committed a lot of extra time for meetings and other reform activities. Some action team leaders did share how hard it was to gather people and to get input from others, and they, definitely, didn't know how to do this in a staff meeting. They were used to staff meetings being driven by a principal who often just gave mandates and announcements. So facilitating meetings was new to them. Sometimes they didn't know how to "take the microphone" from the principal. They needed to learn how to be willing to stand up to their principals and say "As the action team leader I'm supposed to get some info from the other teachers and I'd like to do it in our regular staff meetings." Often, as a faculty meeting progressed, the teacher watched her reform agenda item be continuously moved down the list by the principal. I mean literally moving it down; it might have started right after announcements, and the principal's going on and on and on, and somebody else would go on and on and on, and, suddenly, only ten minutes were left for the rest of the meeting. The principal would say, "O.K., now our action team leader would like to talk to you." The action team leader, of course, did not want to just talk. He or she wanted to engage. Some of those leaders shared with me that "It's hard for me to . . . I don't know how to get my principal to share the leadership with me," and some just said, "I could use some help with facilitation skills." So we created those leadership facilitation seminars, and those really bubbled up from the teachers' concerns and from some of my and the fellows' observations. Those who came really enjoyed, I must say, the skill-building activities even though we hosted them primarily on Saturdays.

From your entire list of team leaders, what was your participation level at the facilitation meetings, leadership skill-building events? Did you have a majority?
Yes, we had a majority. There was one school, however, where a different team leader showed up each time, and that was a challenge.

I'd like to shift the conversation now to parents. What did you, at first, think about parents' roles in schools, just from observing and being in the schools? What did you see as the challenges that parents faced in school reform?

The average parent doesn't seem to know what school reform is other than improving test scores. That's basically what they think it is. I do believe as a result of effective reforms, scores will improve. I'd be the last person, however, if you're looking for somebody to say "We know that we were successful when test scores increased." I'm not going to say it. So that's the first challenge: What is school reform, and how do we know? How do we teach a parent? I think they have to just be engaged enough to get it and feel like they're on the team. I saw that happen in some schools. For too many years parents have not felt truly welcomed, definitely not as decision-makers in the school. If somebody were going to give input as to how a school could be more effective, I would say that was one of the pieces needing immediate attention. As I said before, the prevailing attitude about parents seems to me symbolized in the statement someone very recently made to me, "I hope you're not suggesting that we should be letting parents tell us how to do our job?" I think that because parents have not felt welcomed, often intimidated by schools, they are not willing to engage.

Folami, given that statement you just made, are you suggesting that attitude is true "across the board" about parents, or could it be that there are certain populations of parents that have that feeling of being unwelcome. I'm thinking in terms of the cross-section of schools that we served, and I think specifically of System D. What was your experience of the parents in those three schools?

Wow, it was so different at all three of those schools, and I'll say a little bit about that. I do think there are some interactions between race and class. I find that a wealthier parent seems less intimidated. When her child starts bringing home substandard work, the wealthier parent starts questioning the teacher. That parent will go meet with the principal and talk about the teacher's work and actually document it and look at the difference between Johnny's work from this year and last year and things like that. That comes from the education that a wealthier parent is more likely to have.

For instance in one of the schools from that system, to engage parents the school would host social events for parents, teachers and children, but the Black parents normally would not come. In that particular case, Black parents were from a low-income apartment complex, not public housing but maybe some Section Eight housing. The school hosted a spaghetti dinner that was eight dollars a person. How do you do that if you know and are sensitive to the community you serve? Some families either can't afford the $8 or don't value a PTA meeting enough to pay that amount per person for a spaghetti dinner. There was such an unconscious ignorance about some of the community the school served that some teachers at the school were wondering why many of the Black parents weren't coming. Our challenge was to raise the awareness of these teachers of the issues behind the lack of parental attendance at such functions.

A parent from the economically disenfranchised part of that neighborhood school often doesn't come to such events because she feels out of place. These parents are dressed differently. They often speak differently. They are often used to being told what to do and unaccustomed to just walking up to the principal and teacher and saying something like "You're not effectively meeting my child's needs with your open classroom." These parents sometimes don't know what an open classroom is, don't know much about these various pedagogical practices. It's one thing to feel un-empowered, to not know the jargon, and it's another to have to interact with other parents who don't make you feel welcome. Those were real problems at that school.

At one of the other schools in that district, the same misunderstandings about parents existed. The difference, however, was that a few middle-class African American parents said "I'm mad as hell and I'm not going to take this anymore." They started talking about issues around race and saying we need to take the message to the streets. As you know most Whites don't like you to say race is the issue in a school because they want to say "I'm here to teach all kids, and I'm fair to all kids, and if the parent's not coming, that's not my fault." This school was definitely our race school, and we'll probably come to that in a minute.

Whereas at the school where there was a majority Black population, a school that was very effective, that seemed to meet the needs of the children and their parents, the parents we talked to said they felt their child was loved and nurtured and saw no reason to be at the school because they felt the school served them well. These parents, a majority of whom lived in low-income housing, consistently said, "The school is doing a good job." A middle-class parent, however, is more likely to want to become engaged with the school and see how the school is "doing a great job." These parents would want to see what the school was doing. I think for the most part, though, that the parents at the majority Black school in this system were pleased. They had a sense of community with the school.

Did you see parent involvement shift in any of the schools during those three years that you were involved?

I saw individual parents grow. The more fully engaged parents learned a lot about schools and teaching and the challenges that the teachers faced that the parents really didn't know about before. But I can't honestly say that I noticed at any of the schools where the small core of parents who got to know UACC and who learned new skills as a result of their work with UACC were able to transfer their learning to other parents in any significant way.

Are you saying, then, that while the level of parent involvement did not increase significantly, you did feel that the quality of involvement of some parents increased?

Absolutely.

When you first took on the project as a director, what assumptions did you see being manifested by teachers or principals or anybody in the school community? What assumptions did they make about the possibilities for poor children to pursue academic excellence?

That's a great question. I do remember that you and Lisa and probably other leaders who came up with the proposal or the guidelines for the proposal asked one question of the school, "What are the strengths children bring to the classroom?" And that was a very hard question for them to answer effectively. I believe that's why you all knew it was important to ask it. If educators don't see the assets in their communities, they begin to believe, number one, that they're doing the best they can, and/or, two, there's really nothing else they can do because the students and the parents are the problem, not the school. I think that was a major challenge for teachers and schools. Educators, in general, had some assumptions that children came to school with mostly problems.

I heard the term "crack baby" one time too many. Asa Hilliard has done some research, in fact, on this. It is a misnomer, in the sense of believing that those children operate from a deficit. There are obviously certain impacts on these babies, but these teachers were throwing around "crack baby" and really had no clue what that was. Also they would actually say that these parents don't care about their children. I learned, I mean, I knew it myself, but I saw it up close that parents do care about their kids, even if those parents are never in their child's school.

Who did you hear that the most from, the comments about "the "crack babies" and "The parents don't care about their kids." Did you hear it from teachers? Did you hear it from parents? Did you hear it from principals?

No, I heard that from teachers.

Mostly from teachers?

Yes. I cannot say I heard that much at all from principals, definitely not from a parent. Parents seemed to understand that the problem was a little more pervasive than just that of an individual parent. The parents in these communities seemed to understand that a lot of the challenges we faced were those faced by all in our community, an economically impoverished community where job opportunities are not there because business is not there. Therefore, we spend our own money outside the community. They never articulated the situation in that way. I did, but a lot of parents seemed to understand that.

As you went to the schools, to the meetings, did you notice in any of the schools that some groups of parents were treated differently from other groups of parents?

Yes this is again the intersection of race and class. The answer to your question is yes. If a parent had a college education and used primarily Standard English, teachers seemed to give him more face time, to be willing to really talk about their own challenges as an educator or issues around pedagogy. A teacher might say to such a parent,

"We're using a phonics approach" which they may not have said to a parent who they knew had never gone to college or who did not use a Standard English dialect.

Can you remember any specific examples when you were in meeting, a classroom, or in a school and you actually saw a parent or a student being treated differently from the way other students or parents were being treated?

Yes. I was sitting in the office lobby in a school one day, and there were two parents who were there picking up children, coming to school because of a problem with a child. First of all, they had to wait a long time, and they seemed angry. They were mad because their child had gotten in trouble, and they had to be called away from work. Then they became angrier because they were asked to sit and wait. While there, I saw a parent come in dressed in high heels who had a "girlfriend" kind of conversation with the assistant with no wait. It was very interesting and common also. Sometimes the school might hire a parent, and, of course, that parent was in the "in" group. That parent was treated like a friend, unlike the regular parents and others from the community. I never saw the assistant in the office turn to that parent and say, "I'm sorry you'll have to wait; the teacher is on her way." I never saw the principal or assistant principal come out of their office just to greet the parent. I did see administrators come out from behind, ask an assistant something, and just walk right back in their office and not say, "Hi Mrs., Judy who is your child?" That's a small thing to ask. That was a very vivid memory for me. It truly upset me.

Did you ever address that behavior specifically in the program, maybe, at specific schools where you had observed the problem? Did anybody in the faculty or any one of the parent groups or the action team leaders . . . did anybody specifically address that in any way?

Yes. I do remember one particular school. Several teachers talked about parents not feeling welcome and that it began in the office. I don't remember any resolves. I don't remember any intense discussions about "what can we do about this?" That gets back to the issue of teachers not feeling empowered to ask a principal to change the culture of their office. The office culture is often the principal's culture.

May we shift to a conversation about the university system? What, if any, was the advantage of working within a university system for public school reform? And what were some of the specific disadvantages or challenges?

Well, one of the advantages was access to the tremendous resources in a place like a large university. Some of which we didn't fully take advantage of. However, I do remember having one session on African American history where we used the expertise of professors from the African American Studies Department to help a particular school. I also remember a time when we realized we needed to spend more money and time on evaluation, and we were able to stay right inside the university and pay so much less than what we would have had to pay if we had gone to a research firm. In addition, we were able to use teacher educators, the faculty in different departments within the College of Education, to get involved in the projects in some way or another, whether it was sharing a particular approach to teaching, curricular research and findings, their own expertise in training or research. We got some engagement that was exciting at different moments. We were on to something with people who were doing something at the statewide level. We never really got where I was hoping we would with graduate students who were working at one of the schools. We wanted to begin using what they were learning there to inform the work of the College in its pre-service program. It never went anywhere, but it might have. Four years is just not enough. So that's one of the advantages.

Now that I'm out of academia, I've learned that significant to the culture within an academic setting is the value of taking time to think through a problem. I've noticed in corporate environments, and probably, some non-profits that are running in a more corporate way, the people just want you to do something. They just want you to make a quick decision. Within academia, it is respected that you need to think through it, read about it, have study groups. That was important. We engaged teachers in that intellectual process in a way that was not used in the funded programs that were not university based. We were the only one, in fact, in the country that was university based. I do remember that some of them reminded me more of a United Way or a Carnegie Foundation type of setting that ran more like corporations, where the philosophy is more like, "Here are the steps. OK we have to deliver training, etc."

Rather in UACC, we did the reflective thing and had what I call the "informed discussion." In addition, I don't think the "Unlearning Racism" study group would have ever come out of a project that wasn't university based. Look at how many people were involved who were based in the university who helped make that group happen. The facilitator wasn't in our department at all but heard about it and had done this unlearning racism work in other places. We began reading a book by another scholar. You may recall we had several summer training events that started with reading circles, and so I think that was a tremendously beneficial piece of the university culture that we brought to the schools.

And the disadvantages?

Bureaucracy would be one. Just getting the university fellows' participation approved by the individual departments. That was a joke. Were they really released? Can you think of one that was really released? They were given so little time away from their university duties to work in our schools. Only one seemed able to give her work in the schools the same time commitment as teaching a course. She was in that building every week. When teachers needed help in teaching science, and she knew science, she worked with those teachers. Yet some people said she shouldn't have done that because she worked more like a consultant than a change agent.

We had to spend some time just thinking about who are the fellows and what is the role of the fellows. I guarantee you at some colleges, the fellows' role was just thought of as "One of my professors will be able to make some extra money." I can't think of any school, and I include our home university in this, where we had buy-in from upper level administrators in the School of Education who were excited about learning the lessons from our project that could impact curriculum. I saw you, Joannie, hit your head against the wall just trying to make that happen right here at our university.

Do you think that any inroads were made in that direction? Didn't one of the fellows try to work on connecting some pre-service teachers with one of the schools?

What she did, that was the beginning of what I think we all wanted to see, was she took some pre-service teachers out to the schools.

I think I know what you're saying, that it didn't impact the whole program.

But it did impact her pre-service teachers. They did seem, at least, to begin to understand what reform is. I think teachers who had that experience before starting their first job would be excited about reform. If they got to their assigned school on the first day of school and got a memo about a school reform effort that was going to involve teachers being empowered, they'd be excited about it. Because of their experience as pre-service teachers with a school reform effort like UACC, they essentially would be prepared to welcome change. But for the teacher preparation program to have been affected by UACC, the professor would have had to incorporate it into a curriculum that would be taught when she left.

To your knowledge that never happened?

No, but I can't hold that against the professor. I would say, though, that her chair had no buy-in in our program. The college and the particular school we are talking about had a program in elementary education that was doing some innovative things, was getting a lot of attention from somewhere, I'm not even sure from where, but I do remember the chair just saw this as "Whatever. I got other things going on." Her department has an innovative "Certified in a year program." It was an intense master's program that was a year in school, and then you get to teach and then get your master's at the end of that second year of teaching. The department just never really tried to get its arms around what we were trying to do so that it could support us. At the other large university, the same thing happened. I don't think anybody ever really embraced it. Not the chairs of teacher education programs. I think Carl loved it, but he wasn't over any of the pre-service curriculum. That's a tough cookie. College administration is just a tough cookie. I spent so much time just dealing with the paper work demanded by colleges and universities. Talking on the phone with people going "What is this? And what are we supposed to do with the $5,000?" Some people decided to pay the money directly to the professor without wanting to hear the lessons learned. All I wanted was for all the university fellows to be able to attend some staff meetings at their university of teacher educators and share lessons that they learned and get their colleges to consider something they could do in their classrooms with their pre-service teachers and with their teachers who returned for advanced degrees. I was hoping that the lessons that they learned from the UACC experience in urban schools would inform the work at the university. That was our original plan for involving university professors.

Knowing what you know now through your direction of UACC during its first three years and knowing the outcomes of the projects, what might you do differently if you were to start this project all over again?

One thing I would do differently is engage the leadership in the schools in their vision for the role of a university professor in the building.

The leadership in the public schools?

Right. I don't think we did that enough. We just said, "Here's your university fellow." Before the fellows were even selected, if we had a better sense of what the schools needed and wanted maybe the schools would have understood better the role of the fellow. And the same thing at the university level. We could have gotten buy-in from the chairs of the department that trained pre-service teachers. Maybe they would have assigned the ideal person and prepared up front for ways to take the lessons we learned in the schools and incorporated them into the way they trained teachers with a possibility for a strong commitment to the unique challenges of Urban Education.

I think we did make one really big mistake in spending a lot of energy and training and engaging the fellows. We gave them more in the first year than we gave anybody else. Think about it. They spent the least amount of time in the buildings. I think that was a big mistake. We took them on retreats, two or three retreats. We read as a group. We did many things. I don't know what we were thinking. I think it's because the professors have more time and they like that kind of engagement. Let's be honest, they were our colleagues. So that piece I would have definitely done differently. I would have engaged the school leadership in the same kind of ways, if we could have. Time is always an issue. One thing I would like to do again or differently is get dialogue with some top-level administration in the schools around the substitute teacher idea. The notion of here's the school that wants to actively engage in reform changes and explore best practices, so let's assign a substitute teacher or two to that building. Part of the process is teachers being able to visit each other's classrooms both inside their schools and in other schools while teaching is going on, and, then, be able to stay for a debriefing. Therefore, again that kind of training, support, and nurturing that we initially gave the fellows, I would create for the principals.

We started those dinners for principals. I would definitely do that again. Those principals' dinners were awesome, in a relaxed environment. What I saw Betty Strickland add to those dinners, after the principals knew we weren't there to attack them and blame them, was amazing as well, getting them to read and getting them to think about their own changes that they needed to make as leaders.

If I could put all of what we have to do in reform into two words, I would say we must get beyond blame. That's really big for me, Joannie. For instance, we had a parent and teacher schism. It was time to nurture both groups. We were trying to build support systems within the schools. So the teachers would meet after school or have dinner together, but we wanted to have some structure to these meetings. We began to explore a process called co-counseling, where instead of bringing in a professional counselor, teachers learned to co-council each other. And a lot of it concerned learning to listen.

Initially, we brought in someone to teach us the process. She started talking about the oppression of teachers. I don't think teachers liked that, but they knew it was true. Everything she said was true. She told them, "So this is why we often feel beaten down. But we're going to get beyond blame. We're going to learn to support each other and make each other strong."

That's when she went through one of the key elements of co-counseling, that of having somebody listen to you. She started with asking them to talk about their day within four minutes, and the listener could only nod. She insisted that they show only that they were listening. Not to speak because it changes from listening to judging. This is the story part. For the most part teachers could not talk for four minutes. It was frightening before the four minutes were up to have someone fully engaged in listening to them. If you've been blamed for so long and you've been told to act, you don't know how to talk about your own stuff and feel that the other person is really listening. So you convince yourself you don't have anything to say, and you know good and well, Joannie, that everybody in that room had four minutes worth of dumping to do when the question was asked, "What was on top for you today?" or "What did it take to get here?" You know "To come to the Holiday Inn at five o'clock in the evening after school after packing kids home and whatever. What did it take to get here?"

I say that to say we try to get beyond blaming teachers, principals, parents, the board, the budget, the governor, the university that didn't teach that teacher how to teach and realize that somebody is here because they want to be. We have good intentions and I know good intentions alone will not effectively lead to effectively teaching our children. But it's a beginning just to get beyond blame and realize the school's reforms . . . that it challenges the very foundation that most of us were given as teachers and as students, as children of our parents, and in some cases as parents. It's challenging all of that and that's tough. The bigger issue, that we sometimes talked about but in my opinion not enough, is what the real goals for schools are? Why do we want to teach children? So they could get good jobs? Get an education to get a good job? Or do we want to teach them to be critical thinkers who challenge what exists, who want to create an egalitarian society, who want to build up communities, and not just leave the community with their good job, but transform our world. I know that everybody doesn't think that's what schools should do. But we should at least be able to make that an option for the student who would just run with that idea. I'm afraid that kids have been blamed too for not sitting still, for wanting to run and play, for wanting to go outside at recess.

Were there expectations that you had at the beginning of the project that weren't realized by the end of your participation in the project?

I wanted the action team to be institutionalized and by that I mean I didn't care what they called it. Most schools have a leadership team. I wanted to encourage that action team to be a different group of people than a leadership team. Somehow, however, what we learned about having a decision-making body that felt empowered to take ideas to their principals rarely seemed to compel the action leaders to seriously confront principals on most issues. Teachers, too often, seemed to believe that they could not effect change without the principal's authority. I'm still not sure how we might have surmounted that perceptual obstacle. My thought was always if we could just get the action teams to function in a way that they were truly an empowered group of parents-teachers-administrators and children. We did have a school that put children on the action team. If they had taken those lessons learned and passed them to the existing school leadership team, then, we might have institutionalized a truly empowered, decision-making body in the school. But that didn't happen.

Another expectation I had was that we would be our own expo. We started out by bringing together phenomenal educators to a conference to be in dialogue with our local teachers. It's incredibly amazing that we brought together public and private school educators and didn't make a distinction. In other words we didn't say "We won't bring private school educators because you could never do what they do." I think that was very powerful. I think people liked it. During the Expo, we also had demonstrations with students, and we had so much for parents to do. Parents didn't just have to go to a session on how to be an involved parent; they could go to a session on a new way of teaching a language or discover the purposes and process of a literacy lab. That made them, again, feel that someone respected them enough to engage them. Parents might be sitting next to their child's teacher or their child's principal, learning together, at some of the Expo sessions.

My hope was that not only would schools take those best practices demonstrated at the Expo and begin to incorporate them in their schools but also that school systems would begin to realize they had quite wonderful resources within their own walls and hire those very same teachers as consultants to share their successes and expertise with other teachers within their system.

I think we can be creative and keep thinking outside the box, but I was hoping by year four we'd have an Expo where our teachers, schools, parents, kids would invite the community and their districts to see what they had accomplished. I'd like to believe that something like that will happen.

Beyond these disappointments, however, I know that I learned so much. I'm a better person for doing this, and I still think about running for a board of education. Regardless of the setbacks in the project, I know it was worth the time, effort, and energy. I believe that our teachers in the project became excited about having people listen to them and treat them like the experts that they are. I think that some parents became empowered as a result of working with UACC. I think our principals felt supported and as a result learned a lot from each other and from Dr. Strickland at those dinners we sponsored. I think that all of those who were engaged with the project, teachers, parents, administrators, students learned new skills, new attitudes about urban children and communities, and experienced positive growth because of their participation in the program. Watching so many teachers grow professionally as well as seeing my own growth through this reform process still excites me.

Chapter 3
Betty L. Strickland

Leadership Is Everything

Investing in Professional Development

I want to tell the story of the complexities of working with seven principals in formal and informal settings during the reform effort of the Urban Atlanta Coalition Compact (UACC). Because one of my primary roles within UACC was to mentor these principals, I will lead into their story through a description of my own evolution into a school principal to help the reader understand the perspective I brought with me into the project. In addition, I believe it is important for the reader to understand as well that what I brought to the project was grounded in a lived experience as well as theory. For the same reasons, I will also share my professional story leading into my role as interim superintendent of one of the three collaborating school systems involved in UACC.

During the first two years of the coalition project, I was the deputy director of the Atlanta Public School System (APS) and then the interim superintendent. During the last two years of the project, after having retired from APS, I served as a whole school change coach. These diverse roles gave me multiple lenses through which to view the reform effort. They also allowed me to be aware of the intricate patterns of the many levels of collaborations involved in this particular reform process.

Tender Times: From Caterpillar to Butterfly

My story begins as a neophyte principal whose lonely leadership journey resulted in the transformation of two failing schools: an elementary school in a housing development and a middle school in a mixed-income neighborhood. From the start, the journey was one of struggle to create a learning space for the staff as well as the students. During my work with the UACC, I found myself continuously drawing on my experiences as a principal at these two schools.

The elementary school eventually became a feature on a national TV special about people and places making a difference. The middle school was cited as one of the state's "best schools in the middle for preadolescents."

For a new principal, taking over a failing elementary school in mid-year was an exciting yet scary experience. Having been chosen from among 85 applicants, I came to the site believing that I was prepared for the task of moving the school family forward at a very fast pace. I immediately discovered that my ten years of experience as a teacher, two years as a released teacher assigned to assist faculties in six elementary schools, and two and one-half years as a curriculum support teacher in a middle school had not prepared me for the challenges that I faced as I walked into that building.

The elementary school, located in a housing project two blocks east of the state's capitol, typified an inner-city school in several ways: The facility was old (the building and grounds were dirty, and acts of vandalism occurred almost every weekend); the community was unkempt; and the majority of the students were residents in the two housing developments in the area. The school ranked fifth among the systems' elementary schools whose families were identified as recipients of Aid for Dependent Children (AFDC). Most of the students' potential had not been tapped, as indicated by their achievement scores, and many were cited as undisciplined. Many community members manifested hostility toward me and the school. Teachers were not friendly toward me and, often, unfriendly toward each other. There was clearly racial separation within the staff. Many of the White teachers had been at the same school for 20 or more years and resented a younger Black female taking the helm of "their" school, formerly led by White males, with the exception of a brief three-month period during which a Black male served as principal.

As a first-time principal, my initial reaction to the school climate was one of complete dismay. Once I recovered from the shock, I began to formulate a plan that could possibly bring credibility to the school by making positive, visible yet non-threatening changes to the school climate. My overall goal was to move toward a positive atmosphere in which teachers could teach and students could learn. The first step was to seek ways to improve the building's appearance as well as the attitudes which students, teachers, and parents exhibited.

In order to foster a sense of trust among the staff, I requested from the system's professional development office, a two-week, accredited summer workshop. Unlike most staff development activities at the time, the workshop was planned and implemented by the local school staff. Fourteen teachers fulfilled the requirements essential to receiving increment credit and a salary increase. From my perspective, the primary benefit of the workshop was that of forcing professional and social interactions among the staff and helping the staff to gradually begin to trust me as well as trust each other. As a result of the workshop, subsequent in-service activities were planned on a year-long basis with a printed calendar for each staff member. These kinds of "teachers teaching teachers" workshops, initiated then, were being sponsored 20 years later by the UACC staff for its participating schools.

Recognizing effective communication to be an important skill for improving relationships between the school and community, I reserved each Wednesday evening at 6:00 p.m. for parents who wished to frequent the school and express any concerns they had regarding the school's relationship to the community. The evening hour was selected because during daytime hours at school, I wanted to be free to observe the instructional program and provide support for teachers who were experiencing instructional and classroom management challenges. To maintain and enhance contact with parents, I attended tenant association meetings and other community activities regularly. Another strategy that I found to be helpful during the first few months was that of moving throughout the community and visiting students at home, strategies advocated later by UACC.

To improve student's general behavior and their attitudes toward school, Monday morning assemblies were instituted. Upon arrival at school each Monday, all students would report to the school's auditorium after breakfast. The assemblies served as a transition period in which the students could gradually shift their attention from experiences of the weekend to academics. The first hour of the school week was used to set the tone for learning by conveying high expectations for all students. In addition, the assemblies provided opportunities to:

- use additional human resources to enhance students' learning without disrupting regular class time.
- provide teachers with an extra planning period because elementary teachers had little or no time during the school day for collaboration and individual planning.

One of the most rewarding outcomes of the Monday assemblies was the opportunity for me to teach 546 students directly, demonstrating the fact that every adult at the school was responsible for our children's learning. Another outcome produced by the assemblies was a change in teacher attitudes toward me and each other. They began to work together to plan grade-level units, make suggestions for improving the school, and request assistance from colleagues.

However, many resources and materials were worn and outdated. The media specialist was ill and out on extended leave. At this point, I realized that moving to an improved learning climate was vital. Instinctively, I turned my attention toward two churches in the area. Fortunately, the membership of these mostly White middle- and upper-class congregations readily answered my plea for assistance.

The church volunteers added greatly to enhancing the social climate for staff, from scheduling social activities during holiday breaks to providing incentives throughout the year. As a result of seeing others volunteering, parents became interested and began to inquire as to how they could assist. Many parents made themselves available twice per year to release teachers for brunch or lunch, and many were used as classroom and cafeteria assistants. One parent who was skillful in art became the school's artist in residence and painted a mural on the concrete wall outside the school.

The school put in place numerous activities designed to foster students' growth in the areas of self-worth and individual pride and to encourage community and school pride. Examples included a school garden planted on a section of the school's property and maintained primarily by students and staff with resource assistance from a university extension program; mirror squares placed along stairwells, corridors and in each classroom; and a weekend school-sponsored neighborhood cleanup project.

My mission, as I saw it, was to continue to champion the connection of essential community resources with the school family to help young people successfully learn, stay in school, and prepare for life. Over the years, there were moments that I believed "tender times" would last forever.

However, there was no organized support for me as a new principal, as UACC discovered, a predicament that still persists in many of our schools today. The system's monthly principals' meetings generally provided updates on expectations for reports due. Very little time was spent on professional development or opportunities to collaborate in focused discussions for improving achievement and/or managing administrative tasks. Occasionally, articles would be distributed for later reading and reflecting. In essence, there were no sound personnel practices to assist me in my pursuit to build a professional school community essential for school improvement. As I was struggling to become an effective leader, a review of school improvement literature and intuition provided the impetus for me to continue my journey toward excellence.

June 1981, my new district superintendent (White female) responded in writing after receiving the schools' first-ever yearbook. The letter was a reminder to me of her belief in my ability to make a difference. She stated, "I do not believe that you hear me when I tell you how influential you are. We need you to tell others what you do. Each one, teach one! You see the more principals that we can teach, the more children will be benefited."

Not until two years after the reminder was received, in September 1983, was an opportunity given to let others know what I was trying to accomplish. This opportunity arose after my work as principal was featured on a national television special *New Horizons*. Many of my colleagues, however, were not interested in hearing about special highlighted individuals and/or programs that were found to be making a difference. I had assumed that these experiences, of establishing the system's first church partnership and its exposure as one of the features on a national television special, might open the door to collaboration among us as principals. It became, however, a further alienation of me as a rookie from many of the veteran principals. Though I continued to receive notes of encouragement from the district superintendent, my journey alongside my peers was a lonely one. Later, while working with the reform effort, I witnessed the same alienation syndrome for teachers in the leadership teams of the UACC. They continuously reported to us that many of their peers seemed to resent the new ideas and new successes discovered as a result of their participation in the UACC.

Before my work with UACC, though, my metamorphosis from lonely leader to collaborative leadership began when the APS system's research assistant produced a year-end report (1983), A *Glimmer in the Night*. The report indicated evidence of my school family's success in meeting the system's effective school criteria. This was the most rewarding feedback during my tenure at the school.

Because of that report, I believe, my assignment abruptly changed to that of a middle-school principal in a culturally mixed middle- and upper-class neighborhood, with some students living on the edge of the community in the city's oldest housing project. The move created a greater challenge for me because I was the first female appointed among eleven middle school principals and the first Black principal for that school family.

The middle school faced similar problems to the ones previously encountered at the elementary school: an unkempt building, many staff members who had been in place for more than twenty years, limited social and professional interaction among staff, and no formal plan for school improvement. Unlike the elementary school, however, there were many White and Black parents who were eager to voice the expectations they held for their children. In response, I conveyed to parents my goal of creating a school that focused on enhancing the academic and social development for each student, as well as one that held high expectations for all students, not just the privileged. In an attempt to clarify my vision for the school, weekly communications were distributed to all homes to remind parents, staff, and students that my expectation was that of ensuring an instructional program that was sensitive to all students' lives, one that reflected students' needs. After I made my goal clear, the invitations to dessert hours ceased to appear in my mail stack.

As before, no one prepared me for the challenges that I would face regarding the school climate. My predecessor (White male) left an empty office and no keys. The staff of approximately 70 percent White teachers generally had been assigned White students while most of the Black teachers were left to teach Black students or low-achieving White students.

The newly assigned assistant principal (White female) and I acknowledged the problems with the planned master schedule. Fortunately, being assigned to begin work in August afforded us the opportunity to take action as we developed a new master schedule, before the staff and students arrived. We created a plan that would involve all staff members in positive collaboration, including those beyond the classroom setting. In addition to regular academic teams, we formed four school improvement teams: professional development, special activities for staff and students, environmental concerns, and student discipline.

With six years of experience as a principal, I now realized that the staff would need to take major responsibility for building leadership capacity and, ultimately, school improvement. Although there was much to do, I initially focused on involving all staff in establishing responsible criteria for success and creating a realistic timeline for feedback and evaluation of progress. By the end of my first school year in the middle school, very few complaints surfaced from parents about the quality of instruction students were receiving; teachers were no longer grumbling about typical middle school students; community businesses were eager to become partners; and creditability had been established with parents, students, and staff. Moreover, parents provided the resources and assistance essential to promote academic and social growth.

Renovation progress was extremely slow during the summer break. However, the school climate was much improved despite the onset of construction and renovation at the end of the school year. The district superintendent was provided weekly updates in June and July, but there was no action from the central or district office until August. As much as I wanted to retreat to my cocoon, I remembered that I was committed to the task of ensuring a climate to promote high achievement, and I could not go into hiding.

After touring the building, the system superintendent and his cabinet met with me for approximately only fifteen minutes. They decided that the district superintendent and I would explore possible relocation sites. She and I then met briefly after other cabinet members departed. She suggested that I meet with the newly appointed principal, who also was of African descent, of the neighboring high school to discuss the possibility of our moving in with their school family for approximately four months. Again, I thought of saying, "I am not up to the challenge." Nevertheless, after reflecting on the challenge that our superintendent, Dr. Alonzo A. Crim, kept before us, "being child advocates," turned my thoughts and actions to continuing the lonely journey of creating a team to ensure that *all* students would have equal educational and social opportunities in an atmosphere which promoted excellence.

My district superintendent came to the high school with me to set the tone for my conversation with the principal. Afterwards, the high school staff readily agreed to take whatever action was essential to make the beginning of the new year a success. This was the beginning of a relationship that brought unity to the school families and the entire midtown community. Within three days, we moved into the building with the high school family. Ten classes were housed in the girl's gym while the remainder of our students attended classes in one wing of the school.

One week before Thanksgiving, the associate superintendent informed me that we were to prepare to return to our building on the following Monday. Because the staff and I had become a family and shared responsibility for carrying out our mission of "promoting achievement no matter what," we made the transition back to our building smoothly and never lost a beat.

Living together helped align the middle and high school administrative, teaching, and environmental staffs. They began to plan professional development opportunities together and formed a cadre of teachers who began discussing strategies for improving the academic and social skills of the students that their high school would eventually receive from us. Our effort was the beginning of broad involvement and collaborative reform in our cluster of five elementary, two middle schools, and one high school. There were now eight administrators and several teachers meeting on Saturday to discuss issues and seek solutions to promote higher achievement. One elementary school, the middle school of which I was principal, and the high school were all recognized as state schools of excellence. No longer did I feel lonely in the leadership journey.

Our school received numerous recognitions between 1988 and the 1991-92 school year. Newspaper articles and other media exposure painted a rosy picture of what had been a dim view. The enrollment at our school grew from a population of 350 in 1984 to approximately 800 by 1991.

February of 1992, my assignment was changed to one of providing leadership for eleven principals and their staff. Once again, thoughts of not being able to meet the challenge clouded my thinking until I read the student dedication in the "We've Got The Spirit" yearbook. This dedication was the affirmation that convinced me that the school family and I were on our way to higher achievement.

No more could I revert to my cocoon, for I now had my school family's permission to use my experience in assisting others. Believing in the participatory leadership strategy that was used at the school level, these same strategies were designed to support teamwork within my assigned cluster of schools. I arranged monthly organizational meetings so that principals could direct their own efforts toward collaborative school improvement. The principals' investment in "group learning" seemed critical to improving their effectiveness in individual schools. The group produced a video, *The Principal as Instructional Leader*. Each principal was provided a copy for use within individual schools.

In 1994 my responsibilities increased from eleven to twenty-one schools. Later, in 1996 a new challenge was offered by the system, that of deputy superintendent for curriculum and instruction. In this role, I worked closely with those individuals responsible for assisting schools. Communication and opportunities to collaborate also seemed appropriate at this level.

Just when I thought that I was flying at maximum speed, a different challenge was presented. In 1998, the Board of Education asked that I serve as interim superintendent during their search for a permanent superintendent. Even though my plan was to retire from the system at the end of the 1997-98 school year, I agreed to continue since there was still much to accomplish.

Prior to the beginning of the 1998-99 school year, leadership changes were made at eighteen schools. News of the changes upset many parents who were surprised by the departures of principals they had known for years. There were also principals and board members who found it essential to vent frustration and disappointment over the changes. Never once did my stance change because these reassignments were within my administrative decision-making authority and did not require board approval, as some board members wanted to believe. In support, I felt it essential to make changes in our effort to continue implementation of the system's strategic plan. The plan, "A Community Agenda for Improving Our Schools 1996–2001," was crafted as a guide to accomplishing the system's overall mission, of which staff performance was noted as an area needing improvement.

There were a number of accomplishments noted in the school system's annual summary. Among the initiatives, during my tenure as deputy superintendent and interim superintendent, was the reform effort of the Urban Atlanta Coalition Compact (UACC), a program of the Center for Urban Educational Excellence (CUEE) at Georgia State University. Our school system was among three collaborating systems invited to participate in a partnership with CUEE. The UACC reform effort was supported by an Annenberg Challenge grant and led by Lisa Delpit, renowned author of *Other People's Children*. The program provided opportunities for the system's elementary school families to address programmatic goals and share ideas and leadership strategies for student achievement and total school improvement within their setting and across other project schools. Having served as a member of the advisory committee while I held the deputy superintendent position, I was keenly aware of the benefits that could be derived from school families connecting, interacting, and networking with educational researchers, curriculum planners, and college/university supporters. Furthermore, my personal commitment to the reform effort became even stronger because of my collaboration experience as a middle school principal.

Awaiting my departure and the arrival of the new superintendent, the school year was closed on a positive note. As I left the system, I felt a sense of commitment from the schools to the system's strategic plan. We had begun the journey of involving entire school families in network discussions and efforts to improve teaching and learning. Although I was retiring, there were no thoughts of where my educational flight would take me.

Principal Impact of Principals

Reading Sir Winston Churchill's statement, "We make a living by what we get, we make a life by what we give," was the beginning of the realization that my flight would take me into situations in which I could continue the mission of assisting school leaders, particularly principals, in responding to the challenges they face in their pursuit to bring about whole school change for underserved students in urban settings. Subsequent to a month of rest after retiring, I found myself as a partner in the Center at Georgia State University. The role assigned was that of whole school change coach. What did this mean? How could one individual impact seven schools? I knew that attempting to adequately mentor the administrative staffs of seven schools would demand more time and energy than it was possible for me to give. Such a task would necessitate more than one change coach. The UACC project director and I met to explore how I might work effectively with all schools.

We concluded that one strategy might include facilitation of the principals' dinners, since I had experience as both an elementary and middle school principal. The principals' dinner meetings were begun two years prior to my joining the project. The seven UACC principals gathered monthly to dialogue, study issues, and share ideas for improving schools. In fostering connections, each principal had the opportunity to facilitate a session. On my first visit to the dinner meetings, unfortunately, I observed a great deal of venting frustrations but little to no studying and sharing leadership ideas. Because my initial purpose as a UACC change agent was to support and motivate principals of participating schools through coaching, I was able to shift the monthly gatherings from dinner and unloading individual accumulated baggage to an across-district collaboration and professional growth activity.

The planning process for these new dinner meetings included an information gathering survey in order to determine our blueprint for action. Each principal was requested to respond to questions as to the availability of growth opportunities and leadership connections within their assigned school within the district and across systems. In addition, each principal was asked to provide responses and suggestions as to how UACC support could connect to the overall vision of their school as well as linking professional growth activities across schools and systems. Principals' responses to the survey and their suggestions of strategies to impact whole school change included: more structure during Principals' Dinner; incorporating study groups/best practices; shadowing, cross visitations, and networking to involve principals, assistant principals, and support staff.

The group agreed on an initial idea of focused professional growth activities during principals' dinners. Thus, "More Than Dinner: Food for Thought" became our theme. *School Leadership: Handbook for Excellence*, edited by Stuart C. Smith and Phillip K. Piele (1997), became our reference for text-based discussions along with articles from leadership journals. I hoped that principals would begin to utilize strategies at their local school to empower teachers to lead professional discussions that included reflection, inquiry, dialogue, and discussions.

The principals' dinners provided a sound base to support collaboration within and across districts. As a change coach, I sought to build a meaningful vision of intellectual power shared by all. The group size (seven principals, UACC director, executive and associate director of the center, and me) was small enough to allow for total involvement in a setting free of distraction and intimidation and provided the kind of flexibility essential for problem solving for individual as well as group growth.

My commitment to share my leadership successes and failures with the group when appropriate, I believe, helped develop a nonthreatening environment for positive change. My goal as coach was to be available to support each of the principals in the many environments in which they found themselves daily. I recognized that they, like teachers and students, sometimes require assistance in acquiring attitudes and skills needed to move the school family forward.

I often tell the story of one principal in the group who was difficult to get to know but who made a complete transformation before the end of my first year of working with the group. Initially, when I visited her school, she would not acknowledge my presence. Even though an appointment had been scheduled, I had to sit in the main office for quite awhile. During the office conference, her defense antenna was always poised and ready to attack any idea presented. She would not accept any suggestions. Yet, during one of our last dinners together as a group, she confessed to us that:

> When Dr. Strickland first came to my office, I kept my arms crossed, belligerently listening to her, thinking that the reform meant that my teachers needed to change; my parents needed to change. But after several conferences with Betty, I realized that I was the one that needed to change. So I came out of my office more often and went into teachers' classrooms to observe and advise about instruction. I began to shift from a manager to an instructional leader.

Finally, she said, she began to visualize my role as helping her efforts to help teachers gain the attitudes and skills needed to create an effective school setting. No longer did her teachers meet off campus to strategize as to how to gain power in her school to assist in curriculum decisions that impacted their students. I had encouraged teachers in all of the schools to include the principal in their discussions. Her teachers accepted the idea, and they invited her to attend their leadership meetings. This was the beginning of her willingness to allow me to help her see the complexity of leadership, to feel free to take an intellectual risk by allowing teachers to become more involved in decision-making. Working with this principal became one of the accomplishments that I allowed myself to celebrate. Breaking through the barriers allowed the two of us to reflect and project. Throughout her defensive mode, my role as change coach never changed. There were many clock hours devoted to realizing the goal that had been set for both the principal and myself. At the end of two years, I was convinced that it was time well spent.

Investing in professional development for principals can unleash the fear of failure, provide opportunities for brainstorming ideas for success, and promote the unfolding of victories. I saw the principals' dinners as examples of the power of alternative professional development.

Principals at those meetings confessed that through their dialogue at dinner, they came to the realization that their schools were more alike than different. Several of them said, "Even though our populations are different, educational concerns are similar. Techniques that we're discussing could work in every situation."

At one of the dinners, one of the elementary school teachers said,

Tonight I discovered that I am not on this journey alone. Initially, I came with the preconceived notion that my problems were unique. Networking has certainly enlightened my thinking. The meeting tonight gave me an opportunity to take off my mask and be real in revealing my need for support. The dinners give us an excuse to meet and seek solutions to our problems . . . universal problems.

One of the new principals in this cadre suggested that the dinners gave her an opportunity to ask for advice and support from veterans in times when she did not feel at ease consulting her supervisor in her district. As I, too, had experienced often during my role as principal, several of these UACC principals indicated that their responsibilities as school leaders left them little time to reflect on their practices, to talk with other colleagues about the techniques of leading a school, or to read books and articles about the role of the principal in schools today.

One middle school principal remarked, "This mentoring program serves as a 'breath of fresh air' because it is a time of reflection and learning."

Feedback from principals suggested that they viewed the leadership cohort program as a success. One of the principals said,

The monthly dinner meetings of principals were positive, powerful, and productive. These meetings allowed principals from various districts to come together in a relaxed, supportive, and inviting setting with a focused agenda to address programmatic goals and share ideas and leadership strategies for student achievement and total school improvement. I thoroughly enjoyed the reading and follow-up discussions of professional articles. I found the meetings to be energizing, inspiring, and helpful in minimizing much job-related stress. I needed this support at a time when there was widespread district focus on school reform. The meetings allowed me opportunities to connect, interact, and network with educational researchers, curriculum planners/developers, and college/university supporters. I experienced much professional growth and development through these meetings. Thanks, UACC.

Principals' dinners could not address all of the challenges faced in educating children in urban schools. Rather, the dinners provided opportunities for candid discussions and a glimpse at some of the strategies that were working in schools and the people responsible for leading change in school families. Perhaps, most importantly, the dinners afforded the principals much needed cross-collaboration in the lonely journey to effective school leadership. One of the elementary school principals in her written evaluation of the program said,

Often, the principalship can be a lonely position in a school setting. I found myself anxiously anticipating the meetings so that I would have the opportunity to dialogue with colleagues on the challenging aspects of providing the best possible education for my students. Invariably, I would leave the meetings with renewed vigor and commitment and the belief that it was not an impossible task. The lively discussions on teacher selection, student achievement, parental and community involvement, standardized testing, etc., always provided me with new ideas and strategies which others in the group had found to be effective which also afforded the esteem-building experience of sharing successes I had with my colleagues. The perspectives offered by the researchers, university faculty members, and experienced practitioners were most insightful and provided new opportunities for guaranteed success in my endeavors. The delicious meals were comforting to the mind, body, soul and spirit.

Another principal in her written evaluation said that, "Often, the meetings, held on days when there had been numerous hurdles to overcome, served as a clearinghouse for the seemingly insurmountable problems which can be overwhelming, when one has assumed the mantle of leadership in today's public schools."

Visits to Schools

Follow-up visits to individual schools offered principals additional opportunities, beyond the dinner discussions, to explore new strategies. The visits also gave principals a chance to reveal how they had utilized new understandings and practices learned during dinner meetings regarding leadership for school change. One of the middle school principals asked for UACC support of three challenges she believed her school faced:

1. Finding time and strategies to deal with inexperience of first year teachers,
2. Curriculum alignment with mission and school culture,
3. The curriculum director's limited school administration experience and time constraints due to other duties.

I visited her school two (and sometimes three) days a week to help her address these specific challenges. I conducted staff trainings, advised her in areas of staff communication, staff meetings, and shared problem-solving strategies. In one of her evaluations of the UACC program, the principal claimed that with my support, she was able to implement improvements in each of the three areas:

> Dr. Strickland brought valuable resources that were used by administrators as well as teachers. . . . Because I was able to observe her "approach" and "responses" to school situations, I learned better leadership skills. It was also a huge relief to have an additional person available to respond to the many issues facing middle-school-age students today. With the help of CUEE's staff members present at our school throughout the year, we developed on-going staff development seminars, hand-outs, and in-classroom strategies. Having them [CUEE staff] share their observations and perspectives of students' performances in the classroom and in the school community offered avenues of change for administration and teachers.

The 2001 final report for the UACC program noted interviews with staff from the principals' schools. The interviewees endorsed the program. They reported that the staff appeared more closely knit as a result of total staff involvement. Teacher's roles in the decision-making process increased and allowed them more leeway to experiment within their classroom. One interviewee stated that, "The school had become so focused on test scores that the teachers were afraid to experiment. UACC provided an acceptable vehicle for trying new things. It covered our backs" (*The Atlanta Challenge: Urban Atlanta Coalition Compact, 2001*).

From all indications, leadership capacity-building and direct one-on-one assistance to the principal were enhanced through the principals' dinner meetings and the visits to the schools. Possibilities for sustaining this kind of leadership building were suggested when one of the UACC principals was recognized at a Board of Education meeting. Her school was selected by the state's public policy foundation as a "No Excuses School." Schools recognized by the foundation were schools with high poverty rates whose students demonstrated academic achievement. The practice of "no excuses" can significantly extend the influence of the school into the community, assuring that everyone, principal, staff, parents, and students, assume responsibility for helping students transform from caterpillars to butterflies.

A Former Superintendent's Suggestions for Leadership Capacity-building

I have always believed that neither buildings nor the contents therein make schools effective . . . the people within the school make the difference. In recent years, leadership journals have focused on strategies to increase leadership effectiveness. I believe, however, that the reading of articles alone will not be enough to promote leadership. Central and district administration must create more opportunities for leadership reflection, inquiry, and dialogue in collaborative settings . . . releasing principals from cocoons and supporting them in their journey from lonely caterpillars to a band of beautiful butterflies. My experiences with these UACC principals further confirmed my belief that it is imperative that school systems design professional development programs to support principals in their leadership, capacity-building journey.

It is not enough to say, "Principals must build leadership capacity within the schools to improve student and staff performance." A plan will need to be developed which provides more than lip service to reform. My earlier experiences as a school leader along with my coaching experiences with UACC principals convinced me that a leadership reform plan must:

- Provide principals with one-on-one contact with established school leaders/administrators for purposes of providing assistance, guidance, and support;

- Ensure organized time and opportunities for involvement and cross-collaboration with other principals in similar settings;
- Create forums for principals to collaborate with their peers to foster individual professional growth and development;
- Support strategies that can sustain the development of a school focused "Action Plan," which includes capacity-building and leadership opportunities for teachers, staff, parents, and students, a plan that promotes meaningful change in staff and student performance;
- Demonstrate how to involve all staff, parents, students, community agencies in positive collaboration, including those beyond the classroom setting;
- Require that principals form academic teams and/or school improvement teams within their schools. Examples might include: professional development team, special activities for staff and students team, environmental concerns team, student achievement team, and student discipline team.

My journey with these principals in UACC feels far too expansive to accurately characterize the impact of the project for the principals and the wealth of knowledge that I gained from my experience as a whole school change coach. However, one of the significant lessons for me from this experience was the realization of the quality of life that one can gain, after retirement, from the freedom to give wholeheartedly to one's profession once again, despite the struggles. Serving as a whole school change coach was the ultimate pathway for me to open doors for urban children through the use of my talents, skills, and experience without the constraints of bureaucratic politics that often stifle one's ability to lead.

Seeing the struggles of these principals to make significant changes in their schools, observing their failures and their successes and their attempts to develop collaborative models of school leadership, I was persuaded that in school reform "Leading is everything!"

Chapter 4

One Teacher's Journey with UACC

An Interview with Chinwe Obijiofor

What grade did you teach at the time you were involved in UACC?

First grade, but now I am the reading specialist at an elementary school in another school system. I don't know how my responsibilities will look this year, but last year I team-taught with three different teachers. I went into three different classrooms.

Did you see any positive results from your school's participation in the UACC?

Yes, there were several. Teachers who had not previously stepped up and spoken out or been leaders became leaders. Also, as a staff, we began talking about our school in ways that would move it forward, talking about things that we perceived as strengths and areas that needed improvement. I don't remember having those kinds of discussions prior to UACC. Also, we began asking parents and students what they thought worked in the school and what they thought needed improvement. Those types of conversations were very beneficial.

Afterwards, once we assessed what the reality of the school's performance was, we tried to implement programs that we thought would improve our school. For example, we established a parent program that two of our teachers co-chaired in the beginning. It was a way of trying to get the parents to organize among themselves, talk about what they needed, and get their voices heard. That parent program was successful. Several of the parents attended the "across-district" UACC meetings and retreats and became vocal in the school about issues concerning their children's education. Remember that most of these parents lived in the housing projects across the street from the school.

Can you think of any other positive results?

Those were the main points, and there could have been more if we had not run into some obstacles that hindered our efforts. A major benefit of the project, however, was the support in terms of the workshops, especially the UACC Expo, and the instructional and leadership information we received. Those were also benefits of the program.

Later, I'll ask you to address those obstacles but for now, can you think of any specific workshops, other than the UACC Expo, that were helpful?

UACC sponsored an "across-district" workshop using Professor B's math. After our leadership team attended that workshop, we introduced it to our faculty, and the school adopted that program. It was successful in those classes where the teachers implemented it. Students learned their math.

About how many teachers implemented professor B's process of teaching math?

I am not sure, to tell you the truth. I know there were a few that did implement it, and I was one of them. But other than just me, probably five or six.

You mentioned that there were some obstacles to the project. Could you speak more to that?

The first obstacle was not having the year-long "buy-in" time of the staff. I remember having only two months to look at the program, digest its goals, and buy into it. Because the foundation's funding didn't come through when it was supposed to, the original planning time was reduced, which made it harder to garner school-wide support. That first year, when we really should have been planning the action reform activities, we had to use part of that year educating everyone about the program. A lot of the staff didn't know what UACC was. They only knew that our principal was excited about it, and that a few teachers knew about it and were excited about the project, so the other staff members, teachers, went along with it for those reasons. That's not the same as really buying into it. I think if we had had that full year to educate for "buy-in," we could have spent less time and energy bringing people along during our planning year.

The other thing that I know was a severe hindrance was that we changed superintendents in our second year. When we changed superintendents, our principal wanted to have the superintendent's reform vision as our goals; yet, what we felt was important was somewhat different from what the superintendent felt was important. In fact the principal and I had an argument about this. Her position was that we needed to adhere to the school system's vision because we were under the system's purview. Thus, she believed that what the superintendent had chosen as important issues should become ours. My point was that we had already started down one road. We had already discussed what was important among the staff, parents, and students, and, to a certain extent, what was important to our school. I believed that we needed to continue with the reform that was in the spirit of the UACC program.

I understand her dilemma, though. Because principals are more vulnerable to the whims of the system, I think she had less freedom to buck the school district under a new superintendent. I think that ultimately teachers have more protection than principals when they challenge system mandates.

This dramatic change in the school system became a hindrance to focusing entirely on our school's pre-established UACC reform activities. In theory, the way UACC was set up, I thought, was brilliant. Nevertheless, practically applying it in a school system with a new superintendent became a huge challenge. I don't know how much of UACC the new superintendent was aware of nor how much she had agreed to support it in the schools. I do know the former superintendent had fully committed to it.

All of this meant that in the second year, we changed focus instead of continuing with what we had originally agreed about the direction our school needed to go. I think if we had been allowed more autonomy from our school district, then a lot of things we could have done would have had a stronger impact.

Was this shift a consequence of the new superintendent's mandating other school reform choices?

In a sense, yes. We didn't have that to contend with that during her first year. She didn't introduce school reform during her first year. But what she did say was, "I'm emphasizing A, B, and C." As a result, there were some people in our school who, then, wanted to change our plan of what we thought was needed to fit her A, B, and C. I didn't think we should have changed our plan. I think had our A, B, and C coincided with her A, B, and C, then, okay, go for it. But on the places where they diverged, I believed that we should have stuck with our plan. But, then again, I was speaking as a teacher who had more protection than the principal did.

What do you mean by that?

Because the principal was more easily removed than a teacher. So, ultimately, if somebody was going to be reprimanded, it would not have been me. Even if it had been me, I could hang with it. It would not have been a big deal.

We found that situation to exist with other principals involved in the Project, who had been told their jobs were on the line. What they believed they had the power to support and what they wanted to support often were two different things.

The principal's contracts with the system state that they are responsible for improving test scores. Yet, I do remember that one part of the UACC contract with the school lessened our vulnerability to the pressure of test scores on paper, but those test scores were still in peoples' heads. I am not sure if those UACC agreements with the system and the schools were approved by the new superintendent. I believe that the superintendent's contract with the system was tied to raising test scores. However, without that pressure, at our school we could have gone on with our reform vision and plans. That was the other thing, coming up with a vision that the school supported. That was another stress, something else we hadn't really talked about, our vision as a team.

But you did with UACC?
Yes. We did with UACC.

But before then, you did not have a vision that the whole faculty talked about.
Right.

About how many teachers were on your staff at that time? Would you say sixty?
Well in terms of staff, yes. In terms of teachers, maybe in the forties.

And of those forty, about how many do you think understood what UACC was all about?
I think by the end probably about 80 percent. Now that's not saying that 80 percent or more went along or agreed with it. Maybe even more than that. Maybe even 90 percent.

Would you say that 90 percent were aware of the goals of the project?
In terms of our school plan? Yes. I would say that because each grade level had the goals to talk about and to have input on and to make suggestions to the leadership team.

Approximately how many were totally supportive of your team's vision of change through UACC? Didn't you have a core group at your school who were leading the effort? Approximately how many other teachers, including that core group, would you say understood the goals?
That one I really can't answer because we had teachers whom I'm sure thought UACC was a terrific idea and would have supported those goals wholeheartedly, but you know in education, we have so many things that come and go. So, especially among old teachers who have been teaching for a long time, there's a hesitancy to put themselves fully into something that may not stay around. So it's hard to gauge how many were fully supportive and how many would have been supportive had they not had the cynicism of teaching for so long and seeing things come and go. Then, too, support for our original action plan, as I said, was thwarted by the new superintendent coming in and the school clearly moving towards the superintendent's vision versus what we thought our needs were for our school. Who knows how many of our faculty were impacted by that shift in power, a shift which easily substantiated some of their previous assumptions that reform agendas come and go, so don't take any of them too

seriously. And, too, I might not have received an accurate reading of support because as the UACC chair for the school, well, people aren't going to come up to me and say "This stinks." They are just not going to do that. First of all, we didn't have a lot of teachers with a lot of backbone who would have just done that.

You and a couple of other teachers were the project's faculty leaders of the reform effort. What were some of the challenges that all of you faced beyond the superintendent's change? What specifically at the school did you find created obstacles or just challenges for you?

Well, I am going back to what I said earlier about not having that full year of buy-in time, having to use some of our planning and implementation time for buy-in. I think that was a huge obstacle. I think another challenge was getting people to really understand or believe in how powerful this reform could be, and, as it turned out, I mean they were actually right, it was powerful on paper. It could only be powerful if we had the autonomy to implement it. The other thing is that we sometimes say we want more power as teachers, but not everybody wants the responsibility that comes with that. Responsibly using power is a lot of work. When you go into a decision-making mode and you're responsible for the decisions that you make as opposed to just hearing out somebody else's decisions—that takes extra time and effort. Not everybody wants that. Some just want to do their job and go home. I understand that, but that creates a challenge for school-based change.

I agree. With any kind of change, that seems to be a major challenge. We all would rather just go home.

Yes, that's the challenge. Okay, we have some decision-making power, but with that comes more demands on us. The other challenge was actually finding a way to see ourselves as part of the problem as well as part of the solution. Some people found the physical area in which we worked to be the problem. It is something that happens in teaching. We blame the parents and teachers for a lot of things. As long as the blame is focused on the parents and students, then it's hard to move forward in what you as an individual teacher or as a whole faculty can do. Unconsciously and often consciously, we want the parents and students to change, not ourselves, the teachers.

What, if any, benefits as a professional did you receive as a consequence of participating in the project?

I received many benefits. One of which was actually going to workshops and learning how to effectively facilitate meetings, skills that I learned through UACC which I've continued to use since then. Those were very important skills. I've used them and they have been beneficial in moving change forward in other places. I also went to a workshop on grant writing. I've received grants since then based on the knowledge that I received during those trainings. Those are the two professional gains that stand out, not to mention the networking, meeting other people through the UACC with whom I'm still in contact, people who wanted to change schools to better educate our children. Some of the professional development programs, the training that UACC sponsored, I like many others utilized in the classroom, and I've shared those with other people in other schools. Classroom instruction, funding for a classroom project, facilitation skills, team building . . . all of these were enhanced through my participation in UACC.

What do you think the children in your classroom received as a consequence of your participation in UACC? What benefits?

Well, they obviously received the benefits of the classroom instruction based on the training I received. I think that one of the other things that they received as we, the teachers, got into "un-silencing" our own voices and having more voice at the school level was my understanding that I needed to give my children a bigger voice in the classroom.

You would suggest, then, that some of the strategies that you used in the classroom with your children changed as a result of what you learned in some of these UACC trainings, say the Urban Expo?

Right. My teaching has been African centered for a long time, but I learned specific strategies at the Urban Expo. For example, at the Expo I went to several sessions facilitated by the principal and a teacher from Sankofa Schule, a school in Lansing, Michigan. Afterwards, I incorporated some of their strategies into my instruction. I also went to sessions and bought the curriculum from Roots in Washington, DC. That, too, was effective. I transferred that to my own classroom, and my children benefited through that too.

Is there anything else that you would say your children learned specifically as a result of your being in that project?

Definitely their math computation. It was so on target because we used the Professor B model of mathematics instruction.

I forgot to mention one more benefit for the school and for me as a classroom teacher. As you know one of the things that we adopted as a school (as a result of participating in the Roots workshop or Sankofa's sessions or both of them) was having morning affirmation. Every morning we had affirmation. And that was the total school.

Why did you find affirmations particularly powerful?

Because they set the tone for the whole day as a positive experience. Affirmations seemed to teach children to respect themselves, their peers, their teachers. Saying them also gave them a sense of connection to something bigger than themselves.

Could you explain that practice for some of our readers who may not be familiar with the ritual of spoken affirmations?

Yes, it's the practice of creating and repeating phrases or sentences that affirm who you are as a person, as a group, and/or as a culture. These affirmations often define your vision and/or principles for living a meaningful life. Our students spoke them at the beginning of every day. The purpose of the ritual is to remind us daily that we and our learning or our work have meaning in the world, and that as a people we come from greatness and are directed toward greatness.

You have already addressed this next question in some way, but would you mind addressing any other leadership skills, other than the facilitation and the team building and the grant writing, that you gained from being involved in the project?

Yes. Helping with the school improvement plan, which is one of the things I am doing at my current school. And, at the workshops, I learned the importance of getting people's real input and putting together a school improvement plan.

Often asking for honest input from participants is forgotten, isn't it, or given only lip service?

Yes, very much so. Through UACC, I really saw how important that really, really is.

Other than the benefits that you have already mentioned, besides the different workshops that you attended, were there any other specific events or activities in the project that you thought were particularly useful to you as a teacher or as a leader or a professional?

The monetary support is always important. The workshops were part of the expertise we needed in terms of technical support. It was the expertise that we received, when we were not sure how to do something, then we knew that we had a support mechanism to help us.

When you speak of monetary support, how did that manifest itself? What was the money used for?

The first year, we said that one of our goals was discipline. We believed that our biggest need was improving school discipline. We decided to have the children receive points, when they were at lunch or in a specialist's class such as art, music, or P.E. The classrooms that received the most points (class of the week or class of the month), whoever received the most points in those different areas would receive a special treat at the end of the school year. Everyone who had received a class of the week or month or whatever it was went on a huge field trip. I do remember the "Special Area" teachers saying that when we were on that system, they noticed a marked improvement in behavior. So the monetary support helped, but the thing we wrestled with was how to move from that notion of discipline (that was our starting point) to something more internalized and systemic and less reward oriented. We didn't get to go that route because then we shifted our priorities.

So you would say that the school as a whole was engaged with UACC for only a year before it had to shift its focus?

No, it remained engaged. It was always engaged but it became less of what we had perceived. There was a sense of a loss of autonomy. If the superintendent's agenda had been farfetched, then we probably would have lost engagement, but her focus on attendance and reading was not what we disagreed with. The issues were things we felt we could and needed to deal with. The problem for me was that we had already gone through a lot of trouble, a year of planning and prioritizing and choosing what issues would really move our students forward. Instead of continuing to see where that would go so that we could have some longitudinal progress, the system goals shifted, and so our school goals shifted. Nevertheless, some of our original goals we continued to work toward. For example, we steadily worked toward building better relationships between teachers and parents.

That is a significant change. Did you leave before the project ran out of funding? Or were you there for the whole four years of funding?

I was in the system for the whole four years. I was at another school that last year. I came into a school that had been part of the project, but I was not at that school the other three years to know the dynamics or what had happened before I got there. The principal of that school wanted me to be very involved with UACC, but I don't think there was much going on that last year. It was more like just tying up loose ends. I don't know if the funding was still even there. We didn't go to any workshops or discuss anything. She asked me to write something, but I can't really remember. For the bulk of it I was at the other school.

At your first school, it seemed that the Project's mission was being fully considered.

Yes, we were moving on it. The UACC action team was part of the school's leadership team; so that made it possible for UACC to always be a part of the leadership dialogue. It was always part of what was going on in the school.

One of the benefits of the UACC for parents that you mentioned earlier was their learning to have a voice.

That is the direction we were going in. We asked the parents to meet with us to talk about the goals of UACC. Three other faculty members (Cynthia, Terry, and Priscilla) were co-directing it, and the funds from UACC enabled us to provide child care and dinners during these parent meetings. That was very important because if the parents cannot get child care in the evenings, then they might not come to a meeting. Having dinner for them and their children eased their burden as a parent and became a strong incentive for coming to the meetings. Those cultural pieces were very important, and, I think, the reason we had such a great turnout. It helped. I can speak on this because I attended almost all of the meetings, but I wasn't the director.

The parents were asked what kind of changes they wanted; what they wanted to learn about; and what they needed. After they were surveyed, then the sessions were set up. We hired a facilitator to start it, to begin the first couple of sessions, and then the parents took over. It was set up for approximately four-to-six week initial facilitated sessions. After those, the parents from the first session would be brought in to help train the parents in the second session, so that the leadership was moving from the people who were directing it to the parents. As the sessions progressed, parents would volunteer to design and organize the following sessions. That is how it was supposed to work so that parents would be running it.

We helped instruct them about some activities, for instance, how to meet before the School Board to raise their concerns, practical things. Also, we taught them how to read with their children at home. This was one of the sessions that I led. We gave lots of instruction on improving how they worked with their children at home because that was one of the things they requested in the early sessions. Another of their issues was the food in the cafeteria.

I don't remember much after those first sessions. I know that there were at least two cohorts, two groups of parents who went through six weeks of training. I remember, though, that the parents from the first session helped plan for the second session based on the results of the activities and discussions from the first series of sessions.

Sounds as though many good experiences were created at that school.
Actually, there really were; it just needed to continue. I think that goes back into the buy-in. If people leave who were really out front with it, and there is no time to have the total buy-in, then you end up running a program based upon the leadership instead of the merits of the program itself. The concept of the UACC program, I thought, was a fantastic idea. And I still think it is a fantastic idea.

If you could change anything about the project to make it more effective, what might that be?
The two things I keep harping on. One, make sure that there is an adequate buy-in time, a time for the whole staff to mull over, discuss the concepts behind UACC, really have that time. Then, the time spent on the front end really produces results. I would definitely have that buy-in time even if it limited the time of the actual implementation. It would enable the schools to continue on, for the reform efforts to become self-sustaining. Then I also would have made sure (I don't know if this part is even possible) that the school had the autonomy and the power to continue on with the program. Make it safe for the faculty to continue implementing the vision that the school had set, without having to face the repercussions of the tests when there had not been time

to see the vision fully implemented. To somehow insulate the project from systemic obstacles, those school district barriers that are just part of the school district bureaucracy.

I bought into the concept of UACC, and I still think it is an excellent idea. Having been able to iron out some of the barriers we faced as the new people starting this, I am assuming we were the new people, I think it is an idea really worth pursuing.

What do you think you have learned about the whole notion of school reform as a result of being in UACC? Obviously, you have learned about the buy-in time, that you need that whole year of preliminary work before you even think about implementation. What other things about school reform do you think you have learned?

That reform will only go as far as your school district allows it to go, unfortunately. I guess I really learned how constricted reform can be when you are working within a school system. But I also learned that, through deliberate reform efforts, there is a potential for teacher and parent voices to be stronger and to be heard. Therefore, I believe strongly in pushing for the possibility of loosening those school system restraints because of the strength that we gain as teachers. As I said at the very beginning, I saw people step up to the plate of leadership who I never would have suspected would do so. I never would have even imagined the personal strength manifested by some of those who took on leadership roles. Some of those same people I have seen recently this year, and they are still in leadership positions. They are no longer at the same school, but they are still actively engaged in change, and I think that is a very positive aspect about reform, what it can do for individual teachers and teachers as a group in terms of the decisions that they start making.

Did I hear you correctly when you suggested that through school reform, teachers' voices can be strengthened, thereby opening up the possibility of breaking down the barriers put up by individual districts?

Yes. I really do believe that. I think that once teachers start stepping out, that once they have taken the first initial step (that is the hardest step in terms of speaking out, being a leader, or having some say in decisions being made), they develop a level of confidence. Once they have taken those steps, and that is what UACC enables people to do, they almost cannot turn back to "silence." After we initiated the project at our school, people who previously hadn't really said much of anything were starting to voice their opinions because they suddenly felt that their opinions were valued. Why else would they start when they hadn't previously? Maybe they had spoken among their friends but not to the faculty at large. Once that momentum started, people began feeling more secure and stronger about presenting their opinions in other forms. They started reading more, researching ideas more. They said, "If I am going to be talking about this, let me find out some more about it and become more armed with information." It became kind of a cycle of speaking an opinion and, then, researching the ideas behind that opinion and growing from the experience.

What relationship do you see between teachers being empowered and through that empowerment changing themselves and changing the academic achievement level of the children in the classroom?

When you say empowered, do you mean just in terms of ability to make decisions?

Yes, I guess I am talking about what you referred to as autonomy and gaining a voice.

I think that is one of the factors that ultimately leads to increasing children's academic successes.

With these teachers who you observed find their voices and find their power as professionals, would you say that you saw many of these teachers actually improve their own instruction so that their children achieve academically at a higher level?

I have not seen them, because I left; they left; we have all gone our separate ways. When I have seen them, it has been outside of school settings, where I run into them and ask what they are doing, which is how I know they are still in leadership positions. In terms of what their students are doing academically, I couldn't answer that. I would say that you can have empowerment in terms of having a voice in decision-making but you also have to decide that, "I need to keep abreast of my field, strategies." All of that is important in terms of student achievement. You can have a voice, but if you haven't kept up with your field and what is going on and noticing what works best with your students, then . . . I don't know.

Of course, the ultimate goal of school reform is to raise the academic achievement level of our students. Did you see those possibilities as a result of the instructional strategies that teachers were exposed to in UACC?

Those were definitely possibilities. Before UACC I'm not sure if the entire faculty believed that all of our children could attain academic excellence. During the project we began to know what we wanted for the students.

Are you suggesting that raising the students' achievement level happened for you and for others?

Yes, it happened for me and for others. I saw academic growth with our students from point A to point B. But there is a caveat here because some things that are beyond the school building itself also impact instruction. It is not about blaming parents or children. There is a system in place here. When we say raising our academic achievement, usually it is in relative terms to other people, to students whose parents are able to offer every imaginable support. If there is a benchmark that children are supposed to attain, fine, but I can't see looking at academic achievement always in relative terms to other groups. If a parent can afford a quality tutor for her children or parents who have more economic opportunities available to them can make sure their children get what they need, those children, obviously, have advantages. It is not always a fair comparison to someone who can't afford those opportunities for her child.

That system that you allude to, is that an economic system that creates and sustains conditions of poverty?

Well, yes. The power and economic disparities significantly contribute to the achievement differences.

So as a teacher, what would you say to critics who might suggest that people like Septima Clark, Fannie Lou Hamer, and others from the Southern Freedom Movement taught illiterate sharecroppers to read and write with little to no resources, and, certainly, without parental support? What would be the implications of that for today's teachers?

I would agree that sometimes we as teachers make excuses for poor instruction or simply aren't given the appropriate staff development as professionals to learn diverse effective classroom strategies. I would also suggest, though, that many children from affluent school neighborhoods learn as much from their home environment as they do from their schools. And, if a child from an affluent home doesn't do well in school, his parents have the resources to get for that child what he needs from other professionals outside of school.

You talked earlier about the attitudes and beliefs of some of the teachers about the capacity of poor children of African descent to academically achieve at high levels. Did you see any of those belief systems or attitudes change in parents or faculty?

Let me put it to you this way. They didn't think that poor African American children couldn't learn or that those children have a hard time learning. We obviously had some brilliant children who were performing exceptionally well. The concern seemed to be more about parents who were young, partying, not really paying a lot of attention to their children. I think that was the issue more so than African American parents or children as a whole. It was about specific parents.

I was just thinking in terms of what you had said about some of the teachers blaming the parents or the . . .

Right, and it was true. The other reality, though, was that we had some supportive parents, and, then, there were parents who didn't do well in school so their relationship with the school wasn't positive based on their own experiences as students. Those parents were often viewed negatively if their children were not performing well. Some teachers seemed to see those parents as uncooperative or not doing the things that they needed to do for the success of their child in school.

Would you say that some of those attitudes shifted? Did some teachers see that, possibly, regardless of who the parent was or what the parent was or was not doing, that the teacher could still help that child in the classroom achieve academically at a high level?

I don't know if I observed that attitude change. I think that had we had a longer period of time, that over time, by implementing fully some of the instructional strategies UACC exposed us to, those attitudes would have changed. We would have seen it in the children. Over time we would really have seen a shift because there is nothing like success to get you on the bandwagon. Had we implemented some of the strategies we learned through UACC over a period of time, we would have seen the changes, and that would have changed mindsets about the children.

Do you think, and this is just a hypothesis that I have developed from working with another program involving teachers, that the reverse could be true as well? That a teacher could change an attitude or belief system and, as a consequence of changing that belief system, create academic success with the kids?

Definitely.

Chapter 5
Joan T. Wynne

The Elephant in the Classroom

Racism in School Reform

"Why is it that White women will not raise the issue of racism when engaged in serious conversation about issues that concern us as women?" That question spoken by Mattie Avery,[1] an African American woman, at a women's retreat in Boston has troubled me for several years. At the retreat a small group of women from around the country and two women from other countries had come together to learn strategies for creating and sustaining meaningful dialogue with each other and with other more diverse groups to whom we were connected.

These women and I had spent a weekend together bonding as a newly formed group, experiencing the strategies we were there to investigate, and discussing issues that affect us as women in a world that seems to become increasingly hostile to women and children. Ms. Avery's question emerged on the last day of the retreat, which means that we, the other fifteen women all of whom were White, had been there for two days consciously or unconsciously refusing to raise the issue of racism. Stunned by her question, I puzzled over my part in this group's willingness to remain silent about an issue that impacts every man, woman, and child on the globe. What is it about racism that makes White people assume it concerns only people of color? Why is it that we seem unable to enter into honest discussion about it with each other, knowing that it plagues the planet? And what irony, that fifteen supposedly intelligent and sensitive women had come together to learn new ways of talking openly and honestly about serious issues yet had ignored an issue so fundamental to our personal and societal realities. As a veteran teacher of almost thirty years, I could not help but wonder about the ramifications of those kinds of silences for all of our children in and out of school.

Because of those children in my life, I've sat with Ms. Avery's question for a long time letting it simmer inside of me, wanting to let it go, to keep it from gnawing at me. Though I knew I had raised the issue of racism in all-White circles at other times in my past, I wondered what it was that kept me and the others oblivious to it this time. Avoiding the issue of racism concerns me most because of its consequences on children. I am frankly scared for those children because the political tenor of this country has turned toward a Nazi-like paranoia of all groups of children and adults who are comprised of anything that is not mainstream White Euro-centric. The Internet, radio talk shows, and other media are full of vitriolic condemnations of diverse groups of people. In a 1997 issue of the *Harvard Educational Review*, Bartolome and Macedo echo this same fear:

> The racism and high level of xenophobia we are witnessing in our society today are not caused by isolated acts by individuals such as Limbaugh or . . . David Duke. Rather, these individuals are representatives of an orchestrated effort by segments of the dominant society to wage a war on the poor and on people who, by virtue of their race, ethnicity, language, and class are reduced at best to half-citizens, and at worst to a national enemy responsible for all the ills afflicting our society (Bartolome and Macedo, 1997).

It seems too easy for those of us who think and feel differently about diversity to ignore the need of our voices in rebuttal. Hearing Toni Morrison in a recent television interview say, "When they send the trucks, I know who they are sending them for; they're sending them for me," I understood fully the danger of White people's failure to initiate the dialogue about racism, because I know Morrison is right. In fact, when I look at the statistics showing the disproportionate numbers of African American males in prisons; the disproportionate numbers of children of color living below the poverty level; the numbers of children of color doomed to failure in our public schools; the numbers of inner-city ghettos and Native American reservations, I think we've already sent the trucks. Those trucks in Nazi Germany could have been stopped. One of the factors that allowed them to operate was the early silent global complicity about the persecution of Jewish people. Silence can be dangerous. We have a chance to stop those trucks. We've been silent long enough. As members of the dominant culture, we must say out loud that racism is crippling our nation, ravaging our children, and draining the country of its most precious resource, brilliant human minds.

When I think of our crippled nation, I remember the devastating costs of such silences in the history of this country, during the bloody days of slavery, the days of segregation in the south, lynchings, and brutal, "secret" murders. I think, too, of *The Crucible* (1953), an American play written in the 1950's to remind us of the Salem witch trials. The protagonist, John Proctor, remains silent about the witch-hunts until it is too late, and "murder is loose in Salem." His reluctance to publicly condemn the antics of the children who were leading these hunts allowed women to go to their deaths.

And I think of the McCarthy hearings, the reason Arthur Miller wrote *The Crucible*, and of all the innocents who were damaged by the silence of respectable people who were afraid to call a witch hunt, a witch hunt. I don't think we who understand and have seen the witch hunts of racism can remain silent any longer.

Yet today we are silent about the backlash in California against the children of illegal immigrants. Our people there supported legislation that refuses immigrant children health care and education. Yet these same middle-class and wealthy Californians hire the mothers and fathers of those children to work the soil of mainstream farms, pick their crops, clean their houses, become surrogate mothers to their children. How do we ignore this punishment of immigrant children, knowing that all of us in the dominant culture are ultimately descendents of illegal immigrants in a land originally stewarded by Native Americans? Could it be that in California the Mexicans are coming back to claim the land that was taken from them?

But it is the silence of White women that particularly concerns and confounds me. Concerns me because in the state of Georgia over 80 percent of the teachers in our schools are White women; therefore, if we don't confront the issue for our children in schools, who will ever voice it in the larger context? (*Educate the World*, 1995) When 56 percent of the children expelled from Georgia schools are African American boys, yet they represent only 16 percent of the total school population, how can we remain silent about racism and pretend it isn't a factor? (MRI, 1995) African American students make up 16.5 percent of the national public school enrollment, yet they represent 28.7 percent of children in special education classrooms (*Status of Education*, 1997). With those kinds of disproportionate numbers, how can we excuse ourselves from addressing the issue?

Our silence confounds me because we as women are considered by the larger society to be the nurturers, the protectors of children, the very life's blood of children. Yet here we sit, most of us, in comfort while over 12 million children live in poverty (Shames, 1991). Millions of American children go to bed hungry every night because of a racist system of economics and politics. And too many of us do nothing, assuming the problem is too big for us to tackle. But we can do something. We can educate our students about racist politics and economics, then maybe millions of children won't always go to bed hungry.

Volumes have been written about the damage of educational racism on children of color. The research is replete with our inability to teach these children because of our unconscious racist assumptions about their ability to learn. When serving economically disenfranchised African American children, school systems often assume that because these children are poor and because their culture is different from the mainstream, these students will be unable to achieve academically at the same levels as their White counterparts. Many times without being aware of their own biases, teachers and others who serve these children, operate from a framework of low expectations of success for these children. Assuming that the capacity for learning is somehow hampered by the children's life circumstances, we as educators too often allow these children to get by with less, because less is all we believe they can do. Society in general supports these notions, thus, making it difficult for schools to shift their thinking. Recently, when asked by a local reporter about the possibility of raising the test scores of children in the Atlanta Public Schools, the senior director of the Iowa Test of Basic Skills (ITBS), H. D. Hoover, said that "placing heavy pressure on schools probably will result in higher test scores but he wouldn't trust the validity of those results" (*Atlanta Journal and Constitution*, 1999). He added further that:

> You can't all of a sudden, boom!, turn kids into good readers overnight. Atlanta as a large city district, has all kinds of issues associated with the *nature of kids* and the way they come to school that make things tougher than in a nice suburban community.

Not only is Hoover suggesting that if the test scores are raised, then the system is probably cheating, but also that somehow the nature of inner-city children is flawed. That flawed nature, he insinuates, makes them incapable of making great strides in learning within short periods of time, unlike their mainstream counterparts in those "nice suburban communities."

His racist remarks went completely unchallenged by the reporter. How can we continue to remain silent about the impact of racist thinking on our children when these kinds of notions by supposed experts are routinely espoused in the media as though they were fact?

Nowhere is this thinking more blatant than in the *The Bell Curve*. In that bestselling book, the authors, who get standing-room-only audiences across the country whenever they speak, say:

> People in the bottom quartile of intelligence are becoming not just increasingly expendable in economic terms; they will sometime in the not-too-distant future become a net drag. In economic terms and barring a profound change in direction for our society, many people will be unable to perform that function so basic to human dignity: putting more into the world than they take out. . . . For many people, there is nothing they can learn that will repay the cost of the teaching. (Murray and Hernstein, 1994)

The authors' conclusions about the unworthiness of educating the underachiever, specifically the urban poor, are alarming and certainly underscore the reality of Toni Morrison's perception of the vulnerability of African Americans in our society. With the constant controversy concerning the validity of IQ testing, barring brain damage, how can these authors or anyone else say with authority what a person's learning potential is?

Yet consistently educational experts continue to bombard us with the belief that the learning potential of children of the urban poor is forever limited. In 1997, *Education Week* published an article by Richard Rothstein in which he said that "academic performance of the [Los Angeles] district's students will always be and should always be considerably below national averages." He bases this argument on the supposed fact that "for 30 years, experts have acknowledged that the most important determinants of student achievement are family and community characteristics." As I will share later, the research of many more educational experts has found the absolute opposite to be true. He continues, however, insisting that "children from literate homes with secure economic environments will always, on average, have better academic outcomes than children without these advantages." Therefore, he later concludes that inner-city teachers "who guide their students to the 30th percentile on national achievement tests may bring as much 'value added' to the educational process as teachers in more comfortable communities where students coast to the 70th percentile" (Rothstein, 1997). He, thereby, releases any responsibility for teachers and schools in inner-city neighborhoods to demand excellence from their students because he believes that mediocrity is the best these students can give.

Yet African American scholars and practitioners like Asa Hilliard and Barbara Sizemore (Hilliard, 1991, Sizemore, Brosard, and Harigan 1982) have documented a multitude of effective schools where the majority of students who attend those schools come from single-parent, poor neighborhoods or housing projects yet achieve academic excellence and knock the tops off of national standardized tests. These high-achieving schools produce successful students, despite extreme poverty or dysfunctional home environments. Such schools exist in communities around the country, in Los Angeles, Pittsburgh, Detroit, Lansing, West Virginia, Texas, etc. Many of these schools operate on ridiculously low budgets and limited resources, yet common to all are a firm belief and demand that their children will excel. I find it interesting that few, if any, mainstream scholars ever investigate or cite these schools.

The passages from the current literature that suggest limited possibilities for the children of the poor, especially those of color, illustrate the pervasive and insidious nature of the messages sent by, I assume, well-intentioned educational experts. To suppose that teachers walk into classrooms untouched by these biases is naïve. For many who teach, there seems to be a struggle to, first, believe that all children not only can learn but do learn and are always learning. Whether it be what we want them to learn or not, all children are innately curious and they are in the constant process of learning. And second, it seems to be a struggle for many teachers to believe that they can teach all children. Yet to be a good teacher, both beliefs are imperative before we can expect to be effective in teaching any children. All children, regardless of their socioeconomic status, whether their mother is on drugs or their daddy is in jail, will learn and do learn at prodigious rates. And as long as we believe we can teach them and, therefore, demand that they achieve academic excellence, they will learn whatever it is we want to teach them (Hilliard, 1998). A number of research studies have documented that most children, regardless of socio-economic backgrounds, come to school with the same capacity to learn and at the same performance levels, yet the longer most African American children of the poor are in school, the more they fall behind (Levin, 1988).

This fact seems an indictment of the inability of the school rather than the incapacity of the student.

In 1995, The Educational Policy Research Institute in West Virginia completed a two-year study of elementary schools in their state. The results of the study convinced the researchers that:

> Effective student performance *is* possible despite extreme adverse conditions. In fact, this research identified high student achievement in effective elementary schools irrespective of the degree of poverty, high or low parent education, high or low parent income or high or low parent involvement. (Hughes, 1995)

What makes us pay so little attention to studies such as these?

Hilliard in the 9th Annual Benjamin E. Mays Lecture insisted that "there really is no pedagogical problem to producing academic success among children no matter what their social class, cultural, or gender circumstances may be" (1997).

Because I have taught and worked with teachers in urban schools all of my professional life, like Hilliard, I, too, believe that the fault of low achievement of many children in urban schools lies not with the children but with the educational systems that devour them. I and my colleagues in the Urban Atlanta Coalition Compact (UACC) who were engaged with six public schools in a co-reform effort were exploring ways to create better learning environments for economically disenfranchised African American children. This project was initiated and driven by the research and vision of Lisa Delpit who passionately believes and has documented that poor African American children, like all other children, are brilliant and only wait for us to help that brilliance unfold. Yet, in this collaborative reform effort, whose principal investigator and director were both African American women, we observed that the same insidious messages of racism, repeated by the Rothsteins of the world, played a significant role in the failure of the schools to meet these children's academic needs. However, as Ms. Avery had suggested at the Boston retreat, no one seems to want to name it. No one wants to say the word out loud. As a consequence, I keep hearing Ms. Avery's question ringing in my ear. Why won't White folks raise the issue? Why don't we want to confront it head on? Part of the answer probably lies in the fact that our "White privilege" allows us to benefit from racism—whether we are conscious or unconscious of that privilege. A decade ago, Peggy McIntosh, a White feminist scholar, listed the many societal privileges that she received simply because she was White (McIntosh, 1988). Knowing this to be a reality, however, I still cannot fully answer Ms. Avery. I think there's more at stake than even privilege.

Nevertheless, I seem compelled to explore the question for two reasons. First, my personal history is interwoven in the history of America's racism. I grew up in a segregated South. I rode buses where African Americans sat in the back. I drank from "White only" fountains, and frequented "White only" restaurants. My youth was spent in the midst of Jim Crow laws. My schooling was in all-White classrooms. The second reason is that as an educator, I've witnessed the consequences of racism on children's learning. So the impact of racism on people's lives has been a theme in my life, all of my life.

And I think I've been asking myself Ms. Avery's question since I was eight years old, when I was first visually assaulted by the perverse consequences of the Jim Crow laws. I had returned home one day from my segregated Catholic school and picked up a copy of *Life* magazine from the coffee table. *Life's* camera had caught the images of two six-year-old Black children who, attempting to be the first to integrate a southern elementary school were walking down a street lined on either side with angry White adults. In that same photo, National Guard soldiers stood as the only barriers between those two small children and the hostile bodies of hundreds of grown men and women. What stuns me even now as I bring it back from memory, is the image of the thick, heavy chains that many of those men and women held, threateningly waving them, shouting taunts at those two young but courageous children. Though later in my life, I have read books and seen movies that detailed more horrific depictions of racial hatred, that picture remains the most vivid: the anger, the chains, and the sheer numbers of adults intimidating two vulnerable and innocent children. What in the world could so twist adult human beings that they would want to strike out so menacingly at such small, defenseless beings? With the picture of those chains, *Life* magazine had dramatically captured for me, even as an eight-year-old, the moral deprivation that racism inflicts on the racist, thereby diminishing the whole community. That consequence on the spiritual lives of the privileged seems today as ignored as the debilitating consequences of racism on the lives of its victims—a systemic reality that ultimately makes us all victims, even though some of us materially benefit from it.

But the victimization of children is still my major concern. Too often, while working with the UACC as well as with other projects, I sat at meetings and listened to well-meaning White educators discussing the low academic achievement levels of the urban child. These educators seem sincere in wanting to change that reality, yet they never raise the issue of the impact on classroom instruction of racist assumptions about the capacity of poor children of color to learn. Scholars like Bartolome and Macedo, nevertheless, insist that, "as the end of the century draws closer, one of the most pressing challenges facing educators in the United States is the specter of an 'ethnic and cultural war,' which constitute, in our view, a code phrase that engenders our society's licentiousness toward racism"(1997, p. 223). I, too, believe that it is one of our most pressing problems. So when will we as White educators bring it to the table for discussion?

That discussion drives part of our work in the UACC. In our reform effort, we continue to ask ourselves and our partners to investigate the consequences of racist thinking on the academic performance of urban children. Our work demands that we explore how, as a community of educators who are committed to empowering children to excel academically, we can together confront the issue of racism and class bias in a meaningful way so that our children's capacities for learning are enriched not stifled?

In an article in *Educational Leadership*, Sandra Parks explains our challenge. She said, " Past and present conditions of racism contribute to reduced expectations, opportunities, and resources for students of color who live in poverty. The influences of racism result in policies and conditions that are debilitating for children and young adults, perpetuating rather than reducing the cycle of poverty"(Parks, 1999, p. 18).

In the rest of my discussion I have used the terms culture and ethnicity wherever possible when talking about the issue of "race" because I have been persuaded by the work of a number of African scholars that there is only one race, the human race, and that the "racial" differences among us are actually cultural and/or ethnic. From these studies, I have learned that the construct of different races was developed four hundred years ago to further divide people for the purposes of domination (Carruthers and Harris, 1997). Unfortunately, because the construct of race is so ingrained in the language and in our minds, at times it becomes necessary to use the term "race" to explain people's unconscious rationales for particular behavior.

Patricia Williams suggests that "racism is a gaze that insists upon the power to make others conform, to perform endlessly in the prison of prior expectation, circling repetitively back upon the expired utility of the entirely known"(Williams, 1997). Her definition seemed to manifest itself in some of the UACC schools. There was an insistence in some of our schools during interviews and various program evaluations that what mainstream educators and researchers have discovered as pedagogical truths are universally suitable for all children, regardless of their cultural heritage. There was also an insistence by both White and African American teachers that the children of the poor, especially children of color, have been so "impoverished" by their life circumstances, that we can expect very little from them in academic achievement; and that the best we should hope for is to give them "life skills" and get them ready for jobs.

But, as Williams's definition suggests, our educational success with economically disenfranchised African American children is thwarted because we are "imprisoned" by our expectations of failure for these children. Some of our UACC teachers, as well as many other educators across the country, share a pervasive attitude that there is nothing of merit that these children bring to the classroom; that there is nothing of value happening in their communities; and that any change that happens must happen in the "disadvantaged" children and their homes, not in the classroom and the school. Because what teachers do and know is often unquestioned by them, they assume that the trouble lies in what the students don't know rather than in what the teachers don't know about the students. Therefore, again as Williams's definition of racism suggests, there is a constant circling back to the uselessness of known monocultural strategies and curriculum.

An even bigger surprise, however, than this insistence in education on the pedagogy of the dominant culture, the insistence to do more of what is not working for the urban poor, awaited me as I worked with the UACC. That surprise was the reluctance of mainstream educators to accept the perceptions and experiences of African American scholars. I watched astounded over and over again as White educators ignored the lessons learned by African American scholars whose national and international reputations had been built on substantial research and practices examining how urban children of color learn. Exposed to these scholars' expertise, mainstream teachers and administrators, knowing their schools were failing African American children, still seemed not only to resist but to resent suggestions based on this proven research.

In addition, I was always surprised when local foundations denied funding to such scholars while at the same time making major contributions to White organizations who had no record of success in urban schools. Wherever those decisions were made, I wish Ms. Avery had been there to raise her question. I wish somebody had asked these program directors why they insisted on giving money to unproven White educators to tamper with urban schools where African American children are miserably educated while turning their backs on the work of famous African American researchers with successful track records. How can I reasonably assume that racism, unconscious or not, plays no part in the decisions of these foundations?

Some of my African American colleagues have cautioned me to maintain a balanced view when I look at this thing called racism. They have encouraged me to avoid demonizing White people. I have made a sincere effort to think within those parameters. For I really do believe as Adam Michnik, a Polish freedom fighter once said, "There are no angels, no maggots" (Schell, 1986). Somewhere in our collective histories, there's probably blood on all of our hands. I believe, too, what Parks says, that "learning to face racism and to talk about it transformatively with others requires compassion toward oneself and others" (1999). But when one of my White colleagues suggested I call racism something else when speaking about individuals trapped by it, I began to wonder that if I became too concerned about a balanced view, I might lose sight of the very thing I was trying to get a handle on. If we can't say racism out loud because the word may offend those whom it doesn't exactly fit, then how do we eradicate the disease that's bloodying all of our children? It becomes the "elephant in the classroom" that everybody pretends isn't there. And my experience has taught me that White people want to call racism everything but racism. We will explain it as personality clashes, misunderstandings, over-sensitivity, impropriety, and a hundred other euphemisms. We will call it anything but what it is to avoid recognizing our silent complicity in it. Refusing to call its name reminds me of the military calling missiles, which tear bodies, buildings, and whole cities to bloody shreds, "peace keepers." Our language often masks our hypocrisies. Thus, for my own need to keep myself from abandoning Ms. Avery's challenge, I must say the word aloud, racism.

As Beverly Tatum suggests, institutional racism and White privilege are so imbued in American culture, history, politics, and economics that they become like smog in Los Angeles; if you live and breathe in L.A., you are a smog breather. Living in a racist culture, we consciously or unconsciously breathe in racism (Tatum, 1997, p. 6). Another understanding about racism that is important to grapple with is the impossibility of "reverse racism." Many of us White people whine about this mistaken notion whenever people of color seem to "prejudge" us. Yet if we understand racism as *"a system of advantage based on race [ethnicity]; a form of oppression which is the systematic subjugation of a social group by another social group with access to social power; and that racism = power + prejudice"* (Wellman, 1977), then, I believe we should be able to understand that people of color can be prejudiced but not racist. There is only one culture in this country that has overwhelming power in all of our institutions, and it is not African American. "Every social indicator, from salary to life expectancy," as Tatum says, "reveals the advantages of being White (1997, p. 8).

Because of the ingrained reality of racism in our culture, I also believe that the best we in the dominant culture can be is recovering racists (Feagin, 1997, p. 22). But if we don't come out of denial, we will never be able to be in recovery. Calling ourselves and others racists is, of course, unproductive; however, recognizing our racist assumptions as they unfold is essential. As Probst suggests, if we don't question "culturally established norms," they "become so deeply ingrained in consciousness that they come to seem as substantial and immutable as physical reality itself" (Probst, 1984, p. 67). We become "trapped" by our single cultural lens.

Tatum's and Probst's definitions consistently manifested themselves in the work of UACC. In the earliest discussions of funding for the project, issues of ethnicity arose. In a steering committee meeting when members were discussing the language used in the proposal for initial funding, one of the members, an African American educational consultant, suggested that we take the words "African American" out of the proposal when identifying the children we would target. He said that some foundations might reject the proposal because it specifically designated African American children. A discussion of the efficacy of keeping that description in the proposal ensued amongst the fifteen committee members, a committee comprised of mixed ethnicities, genders, and professions. The committee's conversation ended when one of its members, an elementary school teacher, insisted that because African American children across this country were systematically poorly served in educational institutions, deliberately acknowledging a focus on these children demonstrated an honest attempt to address the problem. That the very naming of the ethnicity of these children could be seen as a problem suggests the power of the unconscious societal agreement to be silent about anything that evokes "race."

When funding finally became a reality for the UACC, we made presentations about the project to the three different school systems who had been contacted concerning their interest in becoming involved in the project. After the central administration of one system decided to invite their elementary schools to apply for the two available slots, I received a phone call from their associate superintendent. He revealed that their board was concerned about the piece of the proposal that designated the target student population as African American. He asked if I would come to the next board meeting to explain the project. This particular board is part of a system in which the majority of students are White and about 40 percent of the students are African American. The district wide test scores indicate that the performance of the majority of the African American students is far below that of the mainstream children. Because of that reality, the central administration, especially the associate superintendent, was enthusiastic about the possibility of our co-reform effort supporting their attempts to change this discrepancy in their ability to teach all of their children. Some of its board members, however, did not want to support the initiative.

Consequently, I attended their meeting and explained the main components of the project. At the end of my presentation, one of the board members, a White female, asked a number of questions about the project. Her major concern about the UACC, she said, was the targeting of one segment of the district's student population. At one point she also asked just what we meant by the term, "children of color." With each question, I attempted to explain the necessity of targeting those children who are least well served by public schools because reform efforts have taught us that if we don't specifically target them, nothing changes for them.

The seven-member board (five Caucasians and two African Americans) eventually approved the proposal with one dissenting vote, that of the White female. Her resistance to citing ethnicity seemed symptomatic of the complicity in this nation to deny the reality of racism. Even with the district's hard data of test scores that reveal its failure to create an environment in which African American children can excel, part of its ruling board still wanted to ignore the reality that issues of ethnic inequities played a major role in the system's incapacity to raise the achievement level of all of their students. Nonetheless, two of the district's elementary schools eventually applied for participation in the UACC.

After all three of the systems approved the proposal for participation in the project, the selection process began.[2] During that process, again issues of cultural differences manifested themselves. Part of the selection process included visits of two or three steering committee members to each of the schools meeting with leadership teams, with random teachers in their classrooms, and with parents. Because we had no director of the project at that time, I visited all of the schools, talking to teachers, administrators, and parents as well as looking at school documents that addressed institutional vision, mission, goals, and records of student achievement. Two of the schools (Peters & Winchell Elementary[3]) that applied have White female principals and mostly White faculties. One of those schools has a majority White student population, and the other has an African American student population.

At Winchell when the African American parent representatives, invited by the principal that day, were interviewed, they complained about their feelings of alienation from the school; of their sense that African American children at Winchell were retained at higher rates than the mainstream children; and of their frustrations that their children were treated differently from the other children at the school (Wynne, 1997). Several mentioned that when they came to visit their children in the school, they felt unwelcome. After the hour's session with the parents, I asked the principal if I could meet with her whole faculty and share the perceptions and issues raised by these parents. My request was based on my need to ascertain the willingness of her staff to address the concerns of their African American parents and to make any necessary instructional or institutional changes. I walked away from that 1-1/2 hour meeting with serious doubts about the faculty's level of awareness of their own ethnic biases. They had spent that hour blaming the parents for being disconnected to the school and for their unwillingness or inability to help the children at home with their studies. In this discussion, the staff manifested a defensiveness about the school's failure to raise the achievement level of their African American students by consistently reminding me of the learning deficits of these children due to their "impoverished" backgrounds and lack of parent involvement, a defensiveness that forced their unconscious racist attitudes to bubble to the surface.

After the meeting, I mentioned to the selection committee my reservations about Winchell's selection. An in-depth dialogue ensued about the efficacy of accepting their application. After a full discussion, it was agreed that the committee would accept them as a partner in the reform effort for two reasons. The first was that the leadership at Winchell as well as the staff had vowed they were committed to school change that would more effectively raise the level of achievement for their African American students. The staff consistently in their interviews acknowledged their need for help in this endeavor. The second reason for Winchell's selection was that the committee believed the school probably reflected the ethnic make-up of a large percentage of schools around the country; and, thus, if the partnership could effect positive change at Winchell, more African American students in the nation might benefit from the experiment.

Once the schools had been selected, the work began. Because the actual monies for the grant were slow in coming, we had to delay the hiring of a director. Thus, I remained intimately involved with the initiation of the project. Our first meeting was a two-day overnight orientation retreat held in early August, designed to build relationship among the schools and universities and to communicate the mission and goals of the project. Fifteen constituents from each school, including parents, staff, and teachers were invited as well as university fellows and district administrators. Most schools sent at least twelve participants. During the retreat it became obvious that everyone there sincerely wanted to raise the academic achievement of the schools' African American students. Cultural differences, however, surfaced immediately as participants responded to the different retreat experiences. The mainstream faculty responded less favorably to experiences that incorporated music and relationship building, feeling those experiences took too much time away from discussion of goals and strategies. While the African Americans responded positively to goals and strategy sessions, they expressed a greater interest than their White counterparts in team-building activities. And three of the majority African American faculties repeated the team-building experiences for their faculties when they returned to school in the fall. These early responses reflected the difference in preferences manifested in the two cultures in the context of the larger society. Wade Nobles suggests that typically, central to the African worldview is the necessity for the sense of relatedness, the belief that "I am because we are," a philosophy that reveres community (Nobles, 1973). The Western worldview is typified by Descartes' notion, "I think; therefore, I am," a philosophy that holds sacred individual rights. Over and again, these two conflicting views played themselves out in the discussions of the individual schools on how they could change to meet the academic needs of their African American students. White faculty often assumed that specific strategies, programs, or more outside tutors were the answer to the problem of low achievement, rarely examining the teacher's relationship to her students as a legitimate means of impacting the achievement levels of these children. In fact, in only one of my interviews with White faculty was the instructional benefit of a personal relationship with students ever specifically mentioned, and this teacher devoted her Friday evenings to spending time with individual students. There were, of course, other instances of White teachers creating classrooms where African American children could excel; however, too many teachers seemed unaware of their inability to connect with their students.

Although manifestations of racist assumptions unfolded during our first year, we were convinced that most of the teachers and staff, both White and Black, that we worked with consciously wanted their African American children to achieve. The fact that they were in denial about any racist suppositions about children speaks to, I think, the pervasiveness of those notions in the larger society, making it all the more difficult for these educators to recognize their own biases. Their failure to see through these assumptions seems to strengthen Tatum's explanation of the power of institutional racism.

Besides recognizing denial, though, what was also important to understand while participating in the work of UACC was another outcome of our racist culture: "internalized oppression . . . believing the distorted messages about one's own group"(Tatum, p. 6). During those first selection interviews, I began to notice that many of the African American teachers had somehow swallowed the racist notions of the dominant culture against their own children. As often is true with oppressed peoples, the distortions of the oppressor become the beliefs of the oppressed. These teachers, too, could be heard blaming the children's low academic achievement on the plight of their parents, on the consequences of their poverty, and on the intellectual damage of these children due to their "disadvantaged" backgrounds. I had come up against this before when working with teachers in other public schools. Once an African American teacher, at a middle school serving children who lived in a housing project, informed me that her class of low-achieving science students could not go to the science laboratory because they could only handle "pencil and paper work." She insisted that they didn't have the social skills needed for laboratory work and, evidently, saw no responsibility to teach them those skills.

As I visited all of the UACC schools, some of the insights I received by talking to their teachers led me to believe that most of the schools' faculties lacked a sense of the potential genius of the children they taught (Delpit, 1997). They consistently talked about the shortcomings of the children, the skills they lacked, the poor neighborhoods they lived in, the lack of appropriate encouragement for schooling from their parents, the consequences of their poverty, the negative impact of their single-parent homes, etc. There was almost always a sense of doom about the chances of these children to excel. In none of the interviews did I hear teachers or administrators mention the strengths of these students. Often during the interview process, after a litany of deficits was proclaimed, I interjected the question: "What are these students' strengths?" Too many times there was complete silence while teachers or administrators struggled to think of some. Moreover, their voices seemed to echo the larger society's notion that the people in poverty, not the economic and political systems, are the cause of their own dilemma.

Because of this propensity of most of the faculties to externalize the causes for the academic failure of these children, I wanted our first Town Meeting[4] of representatives from all the schools to focus on the "Ten Factors Essential to Success in Urban Classrooms"[5] that Delpit had developed. I thought her research discoveries, grounded in building instruction on the strengths of our urban children, their families, and their culture, could inform the individual and collective investigations for school reform. For I knew that her writing and research had worked magic on thousands of educators like me. Thus, I believed a discussion of her principles might help to dispel the schools' general acceptance that poor African American children, as Rothstein insists, could only achieve at minimal levels. After Delpit's talk, however, to my amazement, many of the White faculty and administrators present walked away thinking they had heard her say that only African American teachers could effectively teach African American children. Because I was there and I had heard no such reference or intimation made by Delpit, I asked several of those teachers for the specifics which had given them that impression. None of them could pinpoint any particular word or words. Several mentioned, however, that when Delpit cited examples of teachers who used the culture of the children as part of their classroom instruction, she was insinuating that only African Americans could know that culture; therefore, only they were most suitable to teach their children. The irony of the misconception of these teachers is that Delpit said at that very meeting that some African American teachers don't understand the culture of the urban poor and, thus, are ineffective. She also stated that some White teachers are excellent teachers of African American children.

The repercussions of that same misconception arose again months later when I was teaching a master's methodology course for the university. One of the students who enrolled was a White teacher from one of the UACC schools. On a night when I was explaining the mission of the UACC to the class, the teacher reiterated the same contention, that at the first Town meeting, Delpit had claimed only African Americans could effectively teach African American children. Once again I asked if the teacher remembered what Delpit had said that implied such a belief. The teacher then admitted that she actually had not attended the meeting, but that she had heard a conversation of teachers at her school who insisted that Delpit had voiced this assumption. Because I know Delpit's work well, I know that she sometimes uses the work of White teachers as examples of exemplary teaching. My professional experience in working with her convinces me that she harbors no such belief about the innate incapacity of White teachers to effectively teach African American children. I also know that she insisted on including White educators and other professionals in the work of the UACC as steering committee members, as university fellows, as associate director of her Center for Excellence in Urban Education. The evidence of her amazing openness to the voices of others should have prevented anyone from assuming she held a bias against White educators. The consistent misconceptions, though, reminded me of how easily people's predispositions can distort information heard as discussed in Rokeach's research concerning ethnocentrism:

> Persons who are high in ethnic prejudice and/or authoritarianism, as compared with persons who are low, are more rigid in their problem-solving behavior, more concrete in their thinking, and more narrow in their grasp of a particular subject; they also have a greater tendency to premature closure in their perceptual processes and to distortions in memory, and a greater tendency to be intolerant of ambiguity. (Rokeach, 1960)

His research discoveries again and again became apparent in our work. Because of the unconscious ethnic and class prejudice of many of our teachers, parents, and administrators, research by African American scholars was distorted, ignored, or disbelieved. The propensity of some to stick to the "known" in their problem solving about raising the achievement level of their African American students without exploring the new ideas the Compact offered indicated the trap of their unconscious ethnocentrism.

Shortly after the Town Meeting which was held in November of the first year, the White principal of Peters Elementary, a school with predominantly White faculty and mostly African American students, without consulting her faculty chose to withdraw from the UACC. This principal, Ms. Feldman,[6] was the only principal who had not attended the Orientation Retreat. This may have been a factor in her lack of connection to the work of UACC. One of the major reasons she gave for withdrawing from the project was its divisive quality. She blamed the UACC for splitting her faculty along "racial lines." I have found in my years of work with schools as well as other organizations that when racism becomes obvious to the community at large, the culprit becomes whomever brought it to light, a diversity consultant, a diversity committee, student committees examining the issue, etc. So Ms. Feldman's mistaken source of blame for the divisiveness of her faculty came as no surprise, given that in our early interviews, members of her faculty complained about the division of the staff between White and Black.

Later when I interviewed representatives of Peters Elementary about their exit[7] from the project, that division as well as unconscious racist beliefs about the children surfaced.

One of the White staff, Ms. Smith,[8] when interviewed said, "It broke my heart when the principal made the unilateral decision for the school to end its partnership with the UACC. I, in the beginning did believe, and still do, that the project offered our best hope to change the achievement level of our kids." In her authentic attempt to be fair in her assessment of the reasons for the quick exit, the staff member explained it as a result of mutual misunderstandings and miscommunications between the university partners and the school's administrator and staff. She, however, mentioned at great length, the perception of the White faculty who attended the Town Meeting that Delpit had proclaimed the inability of White teachers to teach African American children. The respondent insisted that the young White teachers had come away from that meeting with the impression that they were "inadequate" as teachers. The respondent also reported that the White faculty kept asking: "After African-centered pedagogy, then what?" She intimated that the African-centered classroom activities suggested by some of the African American teachers as a way of being more responsive to the children's culture seemed inconsequential to the White teachers as a means of teaching "basic skills."

When asked later in the interview if racism had played a role in the demise of the partnership, she insisted that while racism was a societal problem, she felt it had little impact on the problems in her school because "the young White teachers today don't share the prejudices and ignorance that White people of our generation did. They [young White teachers] live in integrated neighborhoods, have shared experiences like "cheerleading camps" with other cultures, are exposed to other cultures more than we were." Though her assumptions here may be accurate, they still do not take in the failure of those kinds of experiences to change institutional racism. No matter the increased exposure of Whites to African Americans, societal racism is still alive, well, and wreaking havoc on children, even if unconsciously so by the mainstream masses.

Ms. Smith's biggest criticism of the project was its invitation to one of Peters's faculty to become a member of the UACC steering committee without first consulting the faculty. She insisted that the administrators of the Compact should have asked Peters's staff to choose a representative from their school, a concern which seemed completely legitimate and a decision that we had regretted immediately after it was made and immediately had rectified. Ms. Smith also insisted that none of the staff would ever have chosen the teacher that we had invited. Nevertheless, knowing that the person selected was African American, and noticing the inordinate amount of time Ms. Smith seemed to want to talk about this decision, I wondered if there were other unspoken issues underlying her comments.

For my initial exit interview, I had deliberately chosen Ms. Smith to interview because she had been with the project from the first orientation meeting, had early on verbalized an enthusiasm for the project, and had actively participated in the work the several months that the school was a partner. I sensed that she was well intentioned and that she sincerely wanted what was best for the children at her school. She seemed, however, unable to recognize the role racist notions about children played in the failure of the school to adequately teach its students, an inability that typified the responses of most White partners in all of the schools.

When I asked Ms. Smith what caused the academic failure of the low-achieving students at her school, she cited the lack of proper nutrition and health care, both prenatal and pre-school, parents' lack of education, poverty, lack of appropriate parental support, etc. There was never a mention of instructional inadequacy, only child and parental flaws. Again her responses were not unique. They typified the assumptions of many faculty members at all of the schools. And as she talked, I couldn't help but remember saying similar things about the families of my "disadvantaged" students almost thirty years ago as a first-year teacher when I taught in an African American high school located in a low-income neighborhood. Had it not been for a group of African American teachers who took me under their wing that first year and taught me how to teach, I might still be saying the exact same words as Ms. Smith. Her comments especially saddened me because I sensed that she wanted her students to achieve yet had no understanding of the insidious nature of the assumptions she held as truth, assumptions that kept her students from achieving. And sometimes I wonder how she could understand when there is such an overwhelming conspiracy by the media and others to keep silent about racism. It was another reminder for me of the necessity to address Ms. Avery's question, and to raise the issue of racism.

Another White teacher who was interviewed at Peters also said that she had walked away from the Town Meeting assuming that Delpit had indicated that only African Americans could adequately teach African American children. Interestingly though, after having heard Delpit's talk, she reported, she bought *Other People's Children* but was still convinced that Delpit believed White teachers could not effectively teach African American children. Like Ms. Smith, this teacher also seemed to love her students, yet, as Rokeach suggested, she filtered new information through her unconscious ethnic prejudices. Unlike many others, though, her interview suggested that she was open to the value of knowing about and using the culture of her children in their classroom.

However, one of the African American teachers whom I interviewed was as surprised as I when her White colleagues misread Delpit. In addition, she related that before the partnership, she believed, the faculty at Peters assumed instruction "couldn't be done any other way" than the way it was already being done. She believed that one of the best things about the partnership was that it got people talking about change. Before the partnership, she said, no one listened to parents, and no one "was used to someone watching what was going on" in classrooms. "All of a sudden," she continued, "when the director of UACC began visiting the schools, it put a different set of eyes on the school; people began to pay attention to what teachers were doing or not doing in their classrooms."

After a number of interviews, it became clear that many mainstream faculty members at Peters Elementary did not want to confront any assumptions of racism. This, of course, was probably not the only reason for the withdrawal. The mutual miscommunications, misinformation, and misunderstandings as reported during several of the faculty interviews suggest that other factors may have played a role. However, the cultural and ethnic tensions that existed among the faculty, which surfaced as they briefly participated in the school's self-assessment, seemed to be a significant factor in the ending of the partnership.

During the first year of UACC, in the three schools where there was a large mix of White and African American faculty, individual teachers and parents, most of whom were African American, confessed concerns about racist attitudes present in their schools to the director and sometimes to university fellows. Yet in larger meetings with the entire faculty, these concerns were rarely raised. This reluctance seemed to echo Ms. Avery's words.

I witnessed such avoidance at a school's faculty meeting called specifically to deal with its first year's evaluation. One of the components of the UACC was the school's self-assessment of what worked well and what did not work well in raising the level of achievement of their African American students. Part of that assessment included the help of "a university fellow" to interview representatives from administration, faculty, students, parents, and staff about their interpretation of the school's strengths and weaknesses. The data were to be used in the school's design of an action plan for school change. At one of the schools, the university fellow asked me to facilitate the meeting while she reported the findings of her interviews and asked the faculty to brainstorm three main themes for school change. Though the issue of racism was reported as a concern of some of those who had been interviewed, when the faculty decided in that meeting on its main themes for school change, it ignored racism as a possible issue to be explored.

A year later, however, this school, with the constant prodding of its university fellow, is now investigating anti-racism workshops for interested members of its faculty, parents, and staff. Though only a handful have voiced interest, it is a beginning.

At the start of our second year of the project, we heard rumors that the school with the predominantly White faculty and students was considering withdrawing from the UACC. The principal, Ms. Jones,[9] shared this decision first with the principal of one of the neighboring UACC schools. When our director learned about it from the other principal, she attempted to contact Ms. Jones to suggest a meeting to discuss the school's decision. It took a number of weeks for the phone calls to be returned. Eventually, though, a meeting was agreed upon. Late in the fall, the director, the university fellow, and I met with the principal to discuss her reasons for ending the partnership. During that meeting the principal related the concerns of her faculty. A major concern, she said, was the African-centered pedagogy recommended by some of the experts who participated in an Educational Expo sponsored by the UACC. The Expo was designed to bring together school staffs from around the country who had proven successful in raising the academic achievement of urban African American children.

These experts were invited to present their "best practices" and educational philosophies to representatives from the UACC schools. The Winchell faculty, Ms. Jones said, believed that some of the African-centered strategies demonstrated at the Expo relied too heavily on memorization and rote drills. The faculty believed that strategies typically supported by UACC lacked opportunities for developing higher order thinking, They maintained this belief even though at the first Town Meeting, Delpit emphatically had said (and illustrated with examples) that "whatever methodology or instructional program is used, *demand critical thinking.*" Her ten factors had also been reprinted in the participants' orientation retreat notebooks (see factor 2 in footnote 5).

Another concern of Winchell's faculty was the UACC's suggestion that the schools use the greatest amount of money from the grant for staff development. Her faculty, Ms. Jones said, felt that they wanted to be free to spend the majority of the budget on after-school tutors to teach the low-achievers to read as well as to use grant money to purchase more reading materials for the students. Their action plans for change seemed to focus on what others could do for these children, outside the normal school day, and on what more or better materials could do.

She also said that her faculty believed that for the amount of money received from the grant, there was too much time and energy demanded. The faculty, she reported, believed that their teaching strategies were sufficient to meet the needs of most of their children and that parental involvement was their major challenge, and, she insisted, they could and were already attempting to accomplish that on their own. Most of their assumptions contradicted the research on effective schools of students with low socioeconomic status. In an extensive study of "unusually effective schools" in Louisiana and California, it was found that:

> The clearest differential between unusually effective [with low socioeconomic status (SES)] and less effective middle SES schools involved a tendency for teachers in the former group to push students harder academically and to take greater "responsibility" for students' achievement than did teachers in "typical" middle SES schools. (Levine and Lezotte 1990)

The insistence of the Winchell faculty to hold to their assumption that they were doing all they could do to help these children achieve, and that only better parental involvement, better materials, or outside tutors could make a difference was a fascinating dynamic. Not only did these assumptions contradict the findings of the research on effective schools, but also they compounded the low academic achievement of their African American students who lived in public housing.

Ms. Jones also mentioned that her faculty was interested in the whole language approach and insinuated that phonics programs were not acceptable to them. Some of the experts at the Expo as well as Delpit suggested that poor children of color, who are not exposed in their preschool years to literate activities, often need a stronger emphasis on phonics than their middle-class counterparts. Most of the current literature on language literacy and the urban poor support these conclusions. The misinterpretation of the Winchell faculty about African-centered pedagogy as well as their assumptions that phonics supporters were arguing against whole language suggested the propensity of us mainstream teachers to either resist the voices or misinterpret the messages of African American educators. We do this even with those educators who have been proven effective with the same students whom this faculty was failing. Although I have lived in the thick of racism all of my life, this particular behavior never ceases to confound me.

Later when the Winchell faculty was individually interviewed, they repeated many of the same beliefs reported by the principal, especially the budget concerns. A number of teachers mentioned the faculty's desire to spend the money received through UACC for more reading materials and more tutors or more computers, indicating again their denial about a need for teachers to change strategies, attitudes about learning potentials, or expectations of achievement. The fault for the low achievement was firmly placed in the laps of the children and the parents. When I asked each teacher what was the cause of the academic failure of their low-achieving African American students, the majority plainly said the lack of parental involvement in the school life of the child and the assumed dysfunctional home lives of children living in the projects. One teacher said "I can't imagine having some of the problems that these children face and coming to school and excelling." The same teacher said, "We've reached a level [with some of these children] where it's not going to go any further." To consciously write off the potential success of anyone who is ten years old or younger astounds me. Nevertheless, many of the teachers shared this same sense of hopelessness for their low-achieving students who lived in the projects.

I asked several teachers, "What would you say to a parent who came to you and said, 'Well, you have my child six to eight hours a day, why do you need my involvement to teach him to read?'" One of the teachers responded that "There's nobody that just six to eight hours a day is going to do it." Another, responding to the same question, said, "Six to eight hours a day is not enough time to do everything with the children. Children need to see that parents value education in their school." These assumptions seem to go unchallenged with most teachers. Even though there is a body of research that indicates that children can achieve academic excellence through instruction during school hours without the involvement of their parents, the pervasive idea is that parental involvement is a necessity for academic excellence. Not only from research studies but also from my own experience with children in housing projects, I have learned that this is absolutely false.

Interestingly, two of the teachers who were interviewed suggested that the faculty assumed that they didn't need to change their instruction:

> I think the other thing is that teachers began to realize that they were going to have to be willing to look at other alternatives from what they had always done. There are just some

teachers over here that aren't willing to do that. They have all the answers and there's just nothing you can teach them. Even if it was trying these with just that one little group. It's sort of like they want something that supposedly works for everybody and if it doesn't it's not their fault. . . . That's not every teacher over here but it's a large majority of the teachers.

This observation of the teacher supported Williams's (1997) definition of racism, of "circling repetitively back upon the expired utility of the entirely known." Often mainstream teachers, as well as others, believe that what they know about instruction is all that anyone needs to know. Thus, if the methods they know don't work, they blame the child or the parent, instead of the instructional practices.

Both of the teachers, who voiced observations about the overall faculty's propensity to stick to instruction that they already knew, seemed to have a better sense of the culture of the African American children in the school than the rest of their faculty. The majority of the mainstream teachers that I interviewed at both Peters and Winchell had difficulty answering the question: "What have you learned about the culture of the African American students at your school?" One teacher, while stumbling over the question, "What are the strengths of your African American children?" blurted out, "Their strength is definitely, at least, they can dance." The other two teachers, however, talked about the power of the extended family of their African American students, the value of the students' involvement in churches, and their talents in "drawing and other cultural and performance arts."

While interviewing the teachers and the principal, I got a sense that the faculty worked hard, thought they were open to change, and sincerely wanted their children to succeed. Yet there was this pervasive feeling of doubt about the capacity of their low-achieving African American children to learn at any higher level. The realities of the home lives of these children seemed to convince these teachers that there was little that they as teachers could do to overcome those life circumstances which the teachers assumed kept the children from learning to read or compute. Their suggestions for school change of more tutors for the children and more involvement of the parents seemed to indicate a belief that teachers lack the power to increase the level of academic achievement for these children. The responsibility and the solutions for these particular children's achievement, the teachers seemed to imply, lay outside their classrooms. On the other hand, their interviews suggested that the teachers had every confidence that their instruction made a difference in the lives of their mainstream students.

Yet the studies in California and Louisiana of "unusually effective schools in low SES" neighborhoods found that "home-school cooperation was weak and parent involvement was 'limited' and that high expectations for students originated largely from the school rather than the 'home and school.'" Our mainstream myth about the children's incapacity to learn without appropriate support from parents is time and again dispelled. The research in the last several decades by numerous scholars like

Delpit, Hilliard, Irvine, Ladson-Billings, Nobles, Sizemore, etc. has indicated that economically disenfranchised African American children, regardless of what's missing in their home lives, can and do achieve academic excellence if teachers expect and demand it of them. Why is it, then, that we in the mainstream keep resisting these documented messages? Is it because the messages come from people of color? The principal and the teachers at Winchell Elementary had all read Delpit's book, which emphasized the need to learn the culture of the children *from the children* and their parents and then bring it into the instruction of the classroom whenever possible. This, of course, is a strategy dependent on developing personal relationships with those students. Her book also stressed the need to include explicit instruction, like phonics, with children who needed it within the context of demanding critical and creative thinking. Again after having read her book as well as after hearing African American educators at the Expo prescribe the same, Winchell's teachers insisted that their method of teaching "critical thinking" and "whole language" was far more valuable. These same teachers had heard and applauded Hilliard when he had spoken to an assembly of all of the faculties in their system about the success of students in classrooms where teachers expected and demanded excellence of all African American children. Nevertheless, the teachers at Winchell, with no empirical data of their own to suggest that their strategies worked for their low-achieving African American children, still chose to ignore the research of these noted African American scholars. They continued what Williams saw as the behavior of racism, "circling repetitively back upon the expired utility of the entirely known." What reasons but racism are we left to consider?

I've heard university educators and others suggest that maybe the reasons for resistance rest in the fact that some teachers just don't want to change. But from listening to the teachers at these schools and observing them in their classrooms, I was convinced that they and the administrators worked hard at what they knew to do, and on a conscious level wanted to change if they thought it could make a difference. But there was the "rub." The teachers' unconscious racist assumptions about the children, the African American children of the poor, drove their expectations and their pedagogy, and their resistance to the voices of African American educators with proven records of success.

At all of the schools, even those who chose to end the partnerships, there were, of course, both White and African American faculty who took time to develop lessons that incorporated the culture of their students. They used creative strategies that built on the interests of the students. In one school a White teacher used movement to teach reading. In another school, a White male teacher used drama and role playing to teach abstract ideas and asked students to develop a dictionary of African American language. In another school where a White and African American teacher were team teaching, their connection to each student in the class manifested itself in a myriad of ways, including the language they used to address their students that signified a caring community of learners. And in one school, the White principal continuously searched for new ways to meet the needs of her African American students. She, from the beginning of the project, admitted with great concern, "We are not giving our Black kids what they need to excel. We need to make serious changes in our school to make that happen." Some of the African American teachers regularly used the culture of the children to teach them new concepts. Two of those teachers at one school said, "We are helping other faculty members learn culturally responsive pedagogy by sharing our materials and strategies." Yet at all the schools, there was a pervasive struggle to transcend societal racist notions about the ability of their poor African American students to succeed.

Through this work with the UACC, I have become even more aware of Ms. Avery's question. Yet I am still no closer to the answer. I have continuously watched as too many of us White people refuse to talk about or recognize racism. I've sat in meetings for hours where we talk about the inadequacies of the education of the urban child, yet we never discuss the role that racist politics, economics, and educational attitudes play in the miseducation of these children. The complexities of their "inadequate home lives" are often bemoaned and the incompetence of some of their teachers, but the consequences of racism in educating children seems never to be raised. As I continue to sit in these meetings, work with public schools, and remember my own silence in Boston, I am convinced that Joseph Feagin, a White educator at the University of Florida, is right when he says, "Most Whites in this country are running as fast as they can from a candid, honest, open discussion of race and racism in the United States"(Feagin, p. 18).

Nevertheless, until more of us of the dominant culture begin to break the silence about racism, my experience suggests that in many classrooms of White teachers and some African American teachers very little will happen to support the academic achievement of urban children of the poor. And in most of those classrooms, it will not be because the teachers don't want these children to achieve. It will be because their unchallenged and unconscious racism thwarts these children at every turn. So I think the first step in allowing these children to excel is our willingness to listen to the children, the parents, and the communities we serve. We also need to begin to listen more attentively to African American researchers, scholars, and teachers who understand the culture of the children we teach and who know how to move these children toward excellence. We need to engage in the kind of listening suggested in Delpit's, *Other People's Children*

> As a result of careful listening to alternative points of view, I have myself come to a viable synthesis of perspectives. But both sides do need to be able to listen, and I contend that it is those with the most power, those in the majority, who must take the greater responsibility for initiating the process.
>
> To do so takes a very special kind of listening, listening that requires not only open eyes and ears, but open hearts and minds. We do not really see through our eyes or hear through our ears, but through our beliefs. To put our beliefs on hold is to cease to exist as ourselves for a moment—and that is not easy. It is painful as well, because it means

turning yourself inside out, giving up your own sense of who you are, and being willing to see yourself in the unflattering light of another's angry gaze. It is not easy, but it is the only way to learn what it might feel like to be someone else and the only way to start the dialogue. (Delpit, 1997)

Though what Delpit suggests can be applicable to all of us when we occupy seats of power, her words are especially significant for White women who teach in the public schools. We must be willing to see ourselves in the "unflattering light" of the stories of our past, the histories of our abuses against people of color as well as the stories of our present privileges. Those realities, along with our positions of power in our own classrooms, demand that we continually examine our racist assumptions, be unafraid to raise the issue of racism, and begin to create safe environments where children can learn about it, talk to each other about it, and learn how to disengage from it. If we refuse to raise the issue, we, then, as Rokeach indicates, damage the development of mainstream children as well, perpetuating the cycle of fear and hostility that cripples the country.

But before we open up the dialogue with our students, we need to talk about racism to each other as teachers. Because White teachers make up the majority of the teaching work force in America (*Educate the World*, 1995) and because racism is damaging the children we teach, we have a responsibility to struggle with it amongst ourselves. We need to discover how to create for ourselves safe spaces for such serious dialogue. Confronting racism head on is uncomfortable and often wrings guilt, shame, anger, or despair from us. We need, therefore, to explore together how to sit with the discomfort long enough to move through these emotions toward a place of healing. But if we continue to wallow in denial about the impact of racism on our children, we can never rid ourselves or society of its abuses, much less begin to heal as a community of humans.

"To suspend our beliefs" about racism so that we can hear the experience of others, especially those of our children, seems imperative. We cannot continue to deny it, be defensive about it, see it as only the problem of people of color. It is our disease, White people's disease. And, thus, it is our responsibility to initiate the conversations. We cannot wait for people of color to raise it. I think they're weary of the conversation. Remarkable educational leaders like Alonzo Crim (Crim, 1991) and renowned scholars like Delpit and Hilliard, all African Americans, don't really talk about racism because it seems to get them and their people nowhere. Instead they spend their energies teaching teachers and the rest of us how to respectfully serve children.

And, I believe, they are right to resist the conversation with White people. In my experience, especially when facilitating diversity workshops, if Black people name it, the Whites in the group simply accuse them of being "too sensitive," of misreading their words or behavior. We White folks seem to think that if we don't use the word "nigger" then we must not be racist. We are crippled by a disease that we can't even call out loud, yet we are drenched in a bloody American history of hundreds of years of racism. Whatever our personal awareness of it, racism still exists as a matter of course in every institution we are associated with. We cannot escape it. As Taylor Branch says in *Parting the Waters*, "Almost as color defines vision itself, race shapes the cultural eye: what we do and do not notice, the reach of empathy and the alignment of response" (Branch, 1988, p. xi).

Many African American educators and parents are busy helping their children heal from the abuses of racism so these children can achieve in spite of it. We can't expect African Americans to heal us. They focus on cradling their communities, creating safe places for their children and families. Yet on some level we all know that if White people don't deal with racism, none of our children will be safe.

Starting the dialogue, raising the issue, is probably the next step after learning to listen to those who have been most damaged by it. And it's a big step since we all know our penchant in the dominant culture for running away from such dialogue. Yet until we address the issue, as Parks suggests, we cannot adequately solve the myriad of problems that emanate from it:

> . . . teen violence, safe schools, gang behavior, drop-out and suspension rates, diversity and equity in personnel policies and school administration, poor achievement among students of color, inequity in school funding, and the needs of children living in poverty. Such school problems directly or indirectly reflect past or present racism and may not be meaningfully remedied until racism is addressed. (Parks, 1999, p. 14)

But after addressing racism, then what? I think the "then what" becomes designing education for all children, White and children of color, as Paulo Freire defined it, as a liberation of the mind, because all children need to be liberated from an education that supports elitism. White children's minds are stunted as well by a system that supports "the pathological contamination of a large body of its clients" (Clark, 1989, p. 33). Those contaminated clients are the children living in poverty, especially children of color. In an educational system where the histories and cultures of Africans, Native Americans, Asians, Latinos, etc., are minimized, trivialized, or completely ignored, everyone's children lose. They lose because all children then absorb a truncated view of world realities, a seriously limited sense of the cosmic whole. In a 21st century world where 82 percent of its population will be people of color (DTH, 1995), how will our privileged White children ever learn to operate in that world if all they ever explore in school is their own cultural truths? How will they understand, much less communicate with those who represent 82 percent of the planet's population? Our ever-expanding global village will demand that they communicate in far more effective ways than most of the present adults in their lives do.

There really are no winners in an elitist system of education. For, ultimately, even at home, the elitist suffers. He is afraid to walk down some of his own streets in the cities he has helped build because he has engineered a permanent undereducated underclass that is angry, and out of that anger, is exploding in violence. That violence is perpetrated not only by some of the angry poor but also, as witnessed recently, by children in middle-class communities. It is practiced as well by the elite, whenever their "knee jerk" reaction to global resolution of conflict is building more tanks, bombs, and missiles to terrorize other countries when the behavior of those countries does not serve "our national interest." If that's the best in "creative problem-solving" that the graduates from our present educational systems can muster, then our schools are cheating all our students. I believe that when education ignores racism, supporting notions of privilege and supremacy, all of our children's minds are trapped into a never-ending cycle of violence.

When I consider the kind of change that our educational system needs to make, I always think of Hilliard's challenge to school systems and university teacher preparation systems:

> Revolution, not reform, is required to release the power of teaching. . . . Virtually, all teachers possess tremendous power which can also be released, given the proper exposure. We can't get to that point by tinkering with a broken system. We must change our intellectual structures, definitions and assumptions; then we can release teacher power. (Hilliard, 1997)

In my work in the UACC, Hilliard's words continuously echoed. It wasn't that these teachers were incompetent. They were quite competent at what they assumed was "correct pedagogy." It wasn't that they didn't want what was best for their students. It was that they were operating out of a system whose "intellectual structures, definitions and assumptions" are based on racist philosophies and epistemologies. Those assumptions prevented them from seeing African American children and parents as real three-dimensional people (not statistics) with brilliant potential. Those philosophies stole the teachers' power. Over and over again when talking to these teachers, I heard intimations of how powerless they felt to teach African American children who live in poverty. The media, educational systems, governmental agencies, probably every institution they were connected to had convinced them that there was little they could do for these children's academic success because their poverty, lack of parental support, or emotional needs had crippled them. The teachers were so steeped in their own unconsciously racist belief systems that they either could not hear or refused to listen to the messages of African American scholars and researchers, messages that could have given them back their sense of power. And by reclaiming the power to teach all children, the teachers, in turn, could empower all children to excel. And then, we'd have our revolution, one where everybody wins.

Maybe the why of Ms. Avery's question about racism is not as important as the question itself? Just asking the question might, at least, initiate a conversation that could lead us to a search for integrity, a wholeness that this country has only dreamed of.

Nevertheless, the "why" of her question still plagues me. But one of the answers to her "why" may have been explained recently in a conversation I had with a friend when Maya Angelou was in town for the Black Arts Festival. I invited my "liberal"

White friend to attend the event with me. After the powerful performance of Maya, I asked my friend how he enjoyed the evening. He said he thought she was quite exciting. I asked him what he liked best about her recitation, and he said it was her humor and her last poem of the night, "And then, I rise." We both raved about those moments in her presentation; and, then, sensing some unsaid dissatisfaction with the night, I asked him what he liked least. And he said, "Her racist comments at the beginning." Surprised at this response, not having heard any racist remarks myself, and believing, as Hilliard suggests, that an oppressed people cannot be racist, I asked what specifically did she say or intimate that smacked of racism. He said that it was her comment that Blacks were in America before Columbus as well as her comments on the racist practices of White Americans. I pushed him further by saying that, to me, those comments didn't represent racism; rather, they represented historical fact. And then he said, "Well, it all made me feel uncomfortable." Continuing to probe, wanting to get at his rationale, I asked him what he thought was the source of his discomfort. Was it really racism or something else? Finally, without any further questions by me, he said "shame." Shame was the source of his discomfort. Shame as a White man "for the hideous crimes against Blacks and Native Americans." In that moment he crystallized for me what for years I have sensed might be at the core of our refusal as White people to address racism.

Maybe it is this shame that many White people don't want to face because we don't know how to go past it. Nothing in the culture teaches us how to experience it and move through it toward conciliation. Unlike many modern psychologists, however, I think there are times when shame is appropriate. When my Euro-centric culture has for four thousand years committed heinous crimes against other peoples of the world, feeling remorse is probably one of the most sane things I can do, that is, if I intend to avoid getting stuck there and, instead, move toward redress. After all, nobody wants to be in a room filled with people stuck in shame.

Nevertheless, during the work with the UACC as I watched people shut down whenever the word "racism" came into the conversation, I thought about the "why" of Ms. Avery's question. My hunch is that unconscious shame could have been at the core of how 15 White women sat silent about racism in that room in Boston. Perhaps, somewhere in our collective unconscious is the memory of how our grandmothers or great grandmothers "forgot" to voice their objection to other women and children being enslaved, beaten, raped, murdered. Perhaps somewhere in our unconscious is the memory that our mothers or someone's mothers paid the women of other cultures slave wages to clean their houses, take care of their children, cook their meals. That, maybe, somewhere in our psyches are the realizations that we, women, continue to pay "illegal immigrants" slave wages to work in our homes and then refuse to allow those women decent health care or their children the right to education. These memories and realizations, if surfaced, would have to create shame. Why else would we keep them so deeply buried? If not, then why are we afraid to explore the consequences of institutional racism on children? How is it that White people come together over and over again to talk about serious issues and rarely, if ever, initiate a dialogue about racism?

If we believe, as do many mystics, poets, scientists, psychologists, and African cultures that we are all one in the universe and are inextricably bound to one another, then we in the dominant culture must own our part in the plight of the oppressed. We must stop blaming the victim of the oppression and look into our own past and present for the responsibility as well as the privileges resulting from racism. Then, maybe, we can move through the shame and into healthy resolution of the conflicts we have unconsciously masterminded.

Like Martin Luther King, Jr. and Andrew Young and all the freedom fighters of the civil rights era, I believe that through confronting racism in our culture, we can begin to "redeem America's soul" (Young, 1996, p. 2).

That redemption, I do understand, will not come from attempts on my part to bludgeon others with the righteousness of any ideology. Righteousness is rarely effective and usually damaging. I also clearly understand that, whatever our culture, we have deep seated prejudices that surface every now and then, uninvited maybe, but very much a part of us. And dealing with that reality is a life-long challenge. To be able to admit to those ugly realities, though, especially those of us who are in the dominant culture, is, I think, the first step toward the redemptive process, a process that makes all children winners.

Notes

1. Pseudonym.
2. Selection was based on signed commitments by the schools that included:
    1. Agreement of school administration to engage in collaborative decision-making with faculty and staff.
    2. Agreement by teachers (80%) to staff development and to engagement in the planning and the implementation process to create an exceptional learning setting for low-income children of color.
    3. Agreement to seek parental involvement and support for this effort.
    4. Agreement to take on the role of a teaching/learning site as a source of assistance for other schools attempting to change.
    5. Utilization of community resources.
3. Pseudonyms for both schools.
4. A gathering of faculty, parent, administration representatives from all seven schools to cross-pollinate best practices and common challenges across districts.
5. Lisa Delpit, "Ten Factors Essential to Success in Urban Classrooms":
    1. Do not teach less content to poor, urban children, but understand their brilliance and teach more!
    2. *Whatever methodology or instructional program is used, demand critical thinking.*

3. Assure that all children gain access to "basic skills," the conventions and strategies that are essential to success in American education.
4. Provide the emotional ego strength to challenge racist societal views of the competence and worthiness of the children and their families.
5. Recognize and build on strengths.
6. Use familiar metaphors and experiences from the children's world to connect what they already know to school knowledge.
7. Create a sense of family and caring.
8. Monitor and assess needs and then address them with a wealth of diverse strategies.
9. Honor and respect the children's home culture(s).
10. Foster a sense of children's connection to community—to something greater than themselves.

6. Pseudonym.
7. EXIT QUESTIONS:
    1. *What do you think causes the academic failure of the low achieving African American students in your school?*
    2. What plans have you or the faculty made to raise the level of achievement of these children?
    3. What parts of the Urban Atlanta Coalition Compact worked well for your elementary school?
    4. What parts of the Compact did not work well for your school?
    5. What have you learned about the culture of the African American students at your school?
    6. What do you see as the strengths of your African American students?
    7. What do you want your African American students to know and to be able to do?
    8. What are some of the staff development needs of your faculty?
    9. What is the involvement of your African American parents at your school?
    10. What plans are being made for more inclusion of these parents in your academic programs?
    11. If you were given extra money to use to enhance your teaching capacity, how would you spend it?
    12. *If you were given extra time to use to enhance your teaching capacity, how would you use it?*
    13. What do you think is the most uniquely beneficial piece of the work of the UACC as it relates to school reform?
    14. What do you think that the UACC could do to be more effective?
    15. How significant a role do ethnic differences play in your school environment?
    16. To what parts of the UACC would you like to continue to be connected?
8. Pseudonym.
9. Pseudonym.

References

The Atlanta Journal Constitution (1999). March 11, p. D3.
Bartolome, L. I. & D. P. Macedo (1997). "Dancing with Bigotry: The Poisoning of Racial and Ethnic Identities," *Harvard Educational Review*, Vol. 67, No. 2, Summer, p. 226.
Branch, T. (1988). *Parting The Waters: America in the King Years 1954-63* (p.xi) New York: Simon & Schuster,.
Carruthers, J. H. & Harris, L. C., editors (1997). *African World History Project: The Preliminary Challenge, Association for the Study of Classical African Civilizations.* Los Angeles, CA.
Clark, D. (1989). "High Expectations." *Effective Schools: Critical Issues in the Education of Black Children* (p. 33). Detroit: National Alliance of Black School Educators.
Crim, A. A. (1991). "Educating All God's Children." *Reflections: Personal Essays by 33 Distinguished Educators.* Bloomington: Phi Delta Kappa Educational Foundation.
Delpit, L. (1995). *Other People's Children,* New York: The New Press.
Diversity Trainers' Handbook (1995). Washington, DC: Multicultural Institute.
Educate the World: Elements of Change, Diversity (1995). Video. Atlanta, GA: Satellite Staff Development, Georgia State University and Georgia Public Television.
Feagin, J. (1997). *Reflections on Education and Race: Examining the Intersections: Select Addresses from the Public Education Network 1996 Annual Conference* (p. 22). Public Education Network.
Hilliard III, A. G. (1991). "Do We Have the Will to Educate All Children?" *Educational Leadership,* 49(1), 31-36.
_____(1997). "The Structure of Valid Staff Development." *Journal of Staff Development.* Spring, Vol. 18, No. 2.
_____(1998). "Characteristics of Effective Teachers." Conversation about his research.
_____(1997). "Tapping the Genius and Touching the Spirit: A Human Approach to the Rescue of Our Children." The Ninth Annual Benjamin E. Mays Lecture, Atlanta, GA.
Hughes, M. F. (1995). *Achieving Despite Adversity: A Study of the Characteristics of Effective and Less Effective Elementary Schools in West Virginia.* West Virginia Education Fund.
Levin, H. M. (1988). "Accelerating Elementary Education for Disadvantaged Students." *School Success for Students at Risk* (p. 213). New York: Harcourt Brace Jovanovich, Inc.
Levine, D. U. & L. W. Lezotte (1990). *Unusually Effective Schools: A Review and Analysis of Research and Practice* (p. 66). Madison, WI: Board of Regents of University of Wisconsin System.
Miller, A. (1953). *The Crucible.* New York: Vikings Penquin Books, Inc.
McIntosh, P. "White Privilege: Unpacking the Invisible Knapsack," Working Paper 189, *White Privilege and Male Privilege: A Personal Account of Coming To See Correspondences through Work in Women's Studies* (1988). Wellesley, MA: Wellesley Women's Center.
Morehouse Research Institute (1995). IT'S TIME. Atlanta, GA.
Murray, C. & Hernstein, R. J. (1994). *The Bell Curve.* New York, NY: The Free Press.
Nobles, W. (1973). "Psychological Research And The Black Self Concept: A Critical Review." *Journal of Social Issues,* 29, 1.
Parks, S. (1999). "Reducing the Effects of Racism in Schools." *Educational Leadership,* Alexandria, VA: ASCD, Vol. 56, No. 7, p. 18.
Probst, R. E. (1984). *Adolescent Literature: Response and Analysis* (p.67). Columbus: Charles E. Merrill
Rokeach, M. (1960). *The Open and Closed Mind.* New York: Basic Books, Inc.
Rothstein, R. (1997). "RX for a New Superintendent: A Hand Up to the Students Not a Back of the Hand to Teachers." *Education Week,* Vol. 17, Issue 42, July 09.

Schell, J. (1986). "Reflections," *The New Yorker*. New York: February 3.

Shames, S. (1991). *Outside the Dream: Child Poverty in America* (p. 5). New York: Aperture/Children's Defense Fund.

Sizemore, B.A., Brosard, C., and Harigan, B. (1982). *An Abashing Anomaly: The High Achieving Predominately Black Elementary Schools.* Pittsburgh, PA: University of Pittsburgh Press.

The Status of Education of Black America, Volume II: Pre-school through High School Education (1997). Fairfax, VA: Frederick D. Patterson Research Institute.

Tatum, B. D. (1997). *Why Are All the Black Kids Sitting Together in the Cafeteria? And Other Conversations About Race* (p. 6). New York: Basic Books.

Wellman, D. (1977). *Portraits of White Racism*. Cambridge: Cambridge University Press.

Williams, P. (1997). *Seeing a Color-blind Future: The Paradox of Race*. New York: The Noonday Press.

Wynne, J. (1997). Field notes.

Young, A. (1996). *An Easy Burden: The Civil Rights Movement and the Transformation of America*. New York: HarperCollins Publishers, Inc.

Chapter 6
Barbara Meyers,
Joanne Kilgour Dowdy, &
Patricia Paterson

Finding the Missing Voices

*Perspectives of the Least Visible Families and
Their Willingness and Capacity for School Involvement*

Family Involvement

Numerous research studies have concluded that children do better in school if parents are involved. Improvements in attendance, achievement, behavior, interest in school, motivation, and school completion rates as well as reductions in pregnancy and delinquency rates have been documented (Becker & Epstein, 1982; Comer, 1984; Christenson et al., 1992; Rutherford & Billig, 1995; Slaughter-Defoe, 1991; Wentzel, 1998). We know that parents demonstrate their involvement at different levels from parenting to decision-making to community advocacy (Epstein, 1995; Raffaele & Knoff, 1999; Slaughter & Kuehne, 1988) and participate in a variety of activities such as parent teacher conferences, volunteering, tutoring, and so forth (Hoover-Dempsey et al., 1987). We also know that some parents are less willing and less capable of being involved (Dauber & Epstein, 1993; Fantuzzo et al., 1995; Fantuzzo et al., 1992). Hoover-Dempsey et al. (1997) delineate a useful framework that may explain some parents' willingness and capacity for participation that includes: (1) the degree to which parents assume responsibility for adopting an educational role and the degree to which that role is affirmed by the community, (2) genuine invitations to participate offered by school and child, and (3) parental need for self-efficacy.

While some parents participate readily, others have reported feeling disenfranchised from the school community for a variety of reasons (Davies, 1993; Henry, 1996; Meyers et al., 1996; Walker, 1993). Some parents have had aversive school experiences of their own that prevent their connecting to schools. Others, particularly low SES minority parents, feel they are perceived to have a lower status than educators (Fine, 1993; Menacker et al., 1988; McCaleb, 1994; Rutherford & Billing, 1995) and that negative stereotyping has cast them as disorganized and dysfunctional (McAdoo, 1981; Moles, 1993) with low academic and behavioral expectations for their children (Clark, 1983). Still others who have a low sense of self-efficacy, perhaps because they have attained low levels of education, may find school intimidating (Davies, 1993; Hoover-Dempsey et.al., 1992).

For others, prevailing definitions of involvement are no longer viable or relevant. For example, Walker (1993) writes about highly involved Black parents in Caswell County, North Carolina (prior to desegregation), who attended monthly PTA meetings particularly because they knew they would have the opportunity to talk informally to teachers about their children. Following desegregation, PTAs provided a forum for school politics, and parent teacher conferences became formalized and scheduled, and as a result, the parents from this same community no longer attended these meetings and would be labeled as "uninvolved."

Discussions about parent involvement in schools occasionally blame parents (Davies, 1993). This is especially true for disenfranchised families. Family members may indeed be involved but may not make their participation public or may participate in ways that are not conventionally accepted or understood (Meyers & Dowdy, 1998; Walker, 1993).

Regardless of the reasons supporting or preventing involvement or the nature of participation, parents themselves agree that they are not as involved as they could be. Nationwide, 40% of parents surveyed stated that they do not spend an adequate amount of time on their child's education (National Commission on Children, 1991). The Goals 2000: Educate America Act called for every school to promote partnerships to increase family involvement. There is evidence to suggest that this reform model has increased parent participation in some schools (Meyers et al., 1996). However, McGrath & Kuriloff (1999) suggest that an unintended consequence of this trend is that it may impose a barrier to minority parent school access as White middle-class parents become increasingly more involved and push for exclusionary policies such as tracking.

Family Role in School Transition

Transitions from one school setting to another are critical milestones for children (Bronfenbrenner, 1979; Elias et al., 1986; Felner et al., 1980; Green & Ollendick, 1993; Leonard & Elias, 1993; Parkes, 1971). The early adolescent child has been identified as particularly vulnerable to stressors as he or she adjusts to new academic and social-emotional expectations upon entry to middle school (Elias et al., 1982; Felner et al., 1993). When youth experience difficulties during the transition from elementary to middle school, they may become increasingly inadequate at developing successful coping strategies, placing them in further jeopardy (Blyth et al., 1978; Felner & Adan, 1988). Green and Ollendick (1993) underscored this inadequacy: "Failure to resolve transitions successfully may impair performance and subsequent social adjustment" (p. 162).

Further, there is a significant reduction in parent involvement at each transition point from elementary to middle to high school (Armento & Henderson, 1999; Baker & Stevenson, 1986; Epstein & Dauber, 1991). A three-year collaborative investigation of transitions identified several factors that promote successful transitions from elementary to middle school. These include communication, cooperation, consensus, and commitment; perhaps the key factor in facilitating a smooth transition for their children is the role of parents (NASSP, 1993).

Rationale for This Study

Research is needed to help explain the persistent dilemma of seemingly uninvolved parents, particularly given that their children are at risk for unsuccessful school transitions and concomitant learning and adjustment problems. John Fantuzzo, writing of his work in inner-city Philadelphia, argued for researcher persistence and ingenuity in designing interventions that include and empower parents (Fantuzzo et al., 1995; Fantuzzo et al., 1992). The interventions must not only be sensitive to a parent's "willingness" and "capacity" to be involved but take into account levels of involvement, parental role and efficacy, and invitation for parents to participate. In this spirit, our research goal was to focus on the least visible families, the "missing voices," and ascertain their perspectives on involvement. This research was carried out in three schools in a small school district in a large urban area. This district was part of a large, four-year co-reform initiative, involving three school districts and six local universities. This coalition was an effort to create excellent educational settings for those children least well-served by the educational system, particularly those economically disenfranchised African American children and their families. Under the umbrella of this larger project, the current investigation took place over two years. In the first year, a needs assessment (seventy-five interviews were conducted, transcribed, coded, and analyzed) was implemented in three schools (two elementary schools and their "receiving" middle school). It revealed, among many issues, that while some families had high visibility in these schools, a substantial number appeared to be either minimally involved or not involved. A crucial concern for the three focal schools was to learn more about family involvement, since it was viewed as an educational priority by all stakeholders.

The research reported in this paper was conducted in the second year of the project. The needs assessment data collected in year one informed the design for year two, which examined the nature of family involvement from the perspective of caregivers, especially during the transition from elementary to middle school. A primary focus and unique contribution of the current research was to extend prior investigations by revealing the perceptions of families who had been labeled as being least willing or having the lowest capacity for involvement. Interviews of caregivers of children in both fifth and sixth grades revealed their understandings of their role in the transition from elementary to middle school.

Methods

Context for this research

The small urban school district, located in the southeastern part of the United States, is comprised of seven neighborhood elementary schools, one middle, and one high school. In 1968 the school system was placed under a court-ordered desegregation plan. Another issue which still strains relations in the community was the decision made in the mid-1980s to include the 6th grade as part of the middle school in order to increase the school's population enough to qualify for federal funds to build a gymnasium. This change was made over the protests of the African American parents who maintained that 6th graders were too immature for closer association with 7th and 8th graders. The results of this history can still be observed today in the relationships among school personnel, students, and parents. For example, in 1998–99 African American parents at the middle school felt the need to establish a Black Parent Group separate from the school's PTA. Further, during the needs assessment, one of the elementary principals arranged group interviews of parents by scheduling two separate meetings: one with primarily White parents in the morning and one meeting with African American parents in the afternoon. No parents attended the afternoon meeting.

One elementary school services 211 children, of whom 63.5% are White, 28.4% are Black, and 12% are multi-racial, with 25% eligible for free/reduced lunches. The other has 233 pupils, 97.3% Black, 2.2% White, with 95.5% eligible for free/reduced lunches. The middle school has 660 pupils who are 62.1% Black, 35.3% White, with 55.9% eligible for free/reduced lunches (Georgia Public Education Report Card, 1997–98). The majority of African American children live in projects administered by the city housing authority, and the majority of white children live in middle-class neighborhoods within walking distance of the schools.

This research on family involvement and school transition was carried out in the context of a larger investigation in which researchers conducted individual and focus group interviews with parents, school personnel, and children; observed classrooms and various school/community meetings, and collected student essays, teacher questionnaires, and other existing records (i.e., attendance, behavioral reports, and grades).

This paper reports findings only from the extensive interviews conducted with caregivers. However, it is important to understand the research milieu in which these data were collected, as our comprehensive two-year involvement with the district helped to shape our data collection methods and ground our analyses and interpretations. For example, prior to completing interviews, preliminary conclusions were shared with community participants for feedback and modifications. This recursive methodology led to further revisions of emergent themes and to more focused follow-up interviews.

Participants

Seven members of a bi-racial research team collected and analyzed data. One African American researcher ensconced herself at a housing project's community center. After months spent establishing trust, she was vetted by a key informant and was able to record the stories of heretofore inaccessible families. Other members of the team used ingenuity and patience in tracking down elusive caregivers (interviewing on busses, intercepting parents at dismissal, and conducting interviews on a walk-and-talk basis). Twenty-six African American parents/grandparents, predominantly female, were interviewed. While the majority of the interviewees were low SES women, a few were well-educated middle-class women. In both cases the voices of the least well-served families of color had not been adequately accounted for in the mainstream conversation about children and schooling in this district.

Data sources

Using the procedures described in the prior section, twenty individual interviews were conducted by the research team. These interviews were semi-structured, required open-ended responses, and were audio-taped (Spradley, 1979).

After the twenty audio-taped interviews were conducted and had been subject to preliminary analysis, there was a second round of discussions with a small group of participants. Then, six additional interviews were conducted and video-taped at the school. These interview protocols were informed by the data obtained from the prior interviews.

Data analysis

This collaborative qualitative investigation used a number of the recommendations suggested by Lincoln and Guba (1985) concerning triangulation, prolonged engagement (2-year period), peer debriefing, member checks, and thick descriptions. Negative cases received in-depth attention, to determine how they might influence categories and findings. The study proceeded inductively with categories and questions emerging from the data and being refined into more focused questions and categories.

After completion and transcription of the 20 audiotaped interviews, each member of the research team read over each transcript, doing preliminary coding based on emerging themes. Using constant comparison (Strauss & Corbin, 1990), each member of the research team collaborated with another member to discuss and coordinate initial codes. The entire team then reanalyzed the data to confirm categories, make final changes, and reach consensus on a coding system. During this process categories were derived from the transcripts themselves. Coding proceeded by consensus among group members, with continuous revision of descriptors. During this period, attention was paid to identifying answers to each of the eight questions on the interview form. Subsequent data from the six videotaped interviews dictated inclusion of additional categories. The coding manual was then revised by splitting and splicing to subcategorize and integrate categories. On the basis of emergent themes, categories were renamed. Negative cases resulted in expansion, merging, and deletion of categories. Transcripts which diverged from the current understanding of the team members were analyzed; negative cases modified both the coding categories and the researchers' emerging understanding of family involvement. Negative cases, for example, resulted in findings about defensive attitudes, ineffective parenting, perceived discomfort in the school culture, and conflicting priorities.

Results

The findings are presented in three sections: community definitions of the problem, community involvement activities, and community-generated solutions.

Community Definitions of the Problem

The community itself recognized many of the problems parents faced. Many families spoke of an awareness of racial dynamics or an atmosphere of institutionalized racism in the schools. Parents described "an awesome undercurrent," "a chilly feeling"; one participant said, "Parents feel out of place in the building, in the meetings, as if they are in somebody's way." These attitudes varied in intensity and explicitness, and participants drew different conclusions about the effects of the racial dynamics. Some families blamed the perceived negative attitudes of the school for their children's problems:

> Like my grandson, he got a real bad temper, and whatnot . . . so his teacher thought he was bad, and his mama really didn't have time to come up to the school like as much as the lady would have wanted her to, so they started thinking that he came from a bad home or whatever, and I think from then on out, he was on his own, like them folks just started thinking that he was bad seed, bad home, bad boy and out of reach. So they just let him go.

Another parent linked school attitudes toward children with school attitudes towards parents: "You see what you have to understand is, our children are viewed as having parents who do not care about them, okay? So therefore, they (the school) treat children any kind of way." However, other parents perceived racism as unjustified and unproductive: "I don't think they keep our kids back because we are low-income housing or because of our income or anything like that, but because our children may not be performing on a level that is meeting the standard of that school."

Involvement and empowerment of both children and families were hindered by a self-identified lack of efficacy on the part of parents and grandparents:

> And a lot of us couldn't help our children with their homework because we didn't quite understand. A lot of us have been out of school for a long time. Some of this homework stuff that is sent home we just don't understand, and we send our child to school the next day, and they don't know what's going on, and we don't know what's going on. A lot of them are failing because there is just no communication.

Speaking of homework, one father described "sitting there for hours trying to figure out what does it mean." Such feelings of lack of efficacy interact with feelings by parents that the schools consider them ineffective parents. Parents also recognize the survival pressures faced by teen parents, grandparents, single parents, and families with physical or psychological problems. One participant identified transportation problems complicated by her health: "I can't. . . . go places by myself . . . sometimes my eyesight goes out . . . I can't walk by myself and I got a problem with my legs." A grandparent explained that she doesn't go to PTA because "at the age I am, I try to work a little bit . . . that (PTA) is really for young folk." A working parent said, "I never really got into the school, PTA and all that, because I always had to work in the day and work at night . . . I always had to work two jobs." A grandparent pointed out that "We have a lot of single parents, women who are coming off welfare, can't leave their jobs. I can recommend what they can do, but it's hard." However, most of these families do not offer their problems as excuses, and, in fact, they do go to the school to negotiate issues they see as vital to their children. In response to a request from the school, the parent with vision and leg problems, whose husband was in the hospital at the time, attended a conference with the teacher about her child.

Community Involvement Activities

To offset the problems outlined above, many parents subscribed to the village concept of community characterized by unity, shared parenting, corrective action, and extended family. Participants did not see themselves as alone in the struggle, believing that their concept of strength in numbers could be utilized to support their children and one another: "It takes all of the parents to help each other, and you can do a lot of things without being at the school all the time. You can car pool, or try to fund-raise, or what-ever." Another parent suggested, "If your child is the same age and the same grade, if you live in the community here, if you can find out well, who's going to that event, well, let's go together. You know, encourage one another. . . ." Moreover, families saw that their unity could foster feelings of inclusion in the school and affect the school's treatment of their children:

> And Black parents need to *claim* what it is they need from this school. That's one thing I think that needs to happen. And then White parents have to understand that this school is not just here to serve *their* children. It's here to serve *all* children.

The unified strength of the community extended to shared parenting responsibilities, with community members acting as "adoptive" parents for children whose parents were perceived to be weak in parenting skills: "It would even be good where parents aren't able to come, maybe, or having problems as far as drugs and alcohol, hey, you go up and be a spokesperson for that child." A grandparent indicated the communal nature of her parenting concept: "I'm concerned about all kids. Jamal is my child, but they are all my children." Because of their shared status as insiders, members of the community also attempted to influence parenting behaviors of others. One active parent attributed her involvement to her sister's "forcing the issue" and her sister, brother, and nephew's "pulling for" her and her child. Another parent talked of trying to convince another community mother: "You know, you should stop going to the club on Wednesday night. . . . you could get up there (to the school) and see what's going on with your child."

Parents who faced obstacles such as single parenthood, multiple jobs, or lack of efficacy drew on the combined resources of the extended family to help their children: "Each night of the week I have a night for tutoring, their daddy has a night for tutoring, my niece has a night for tutoring; my sister has a night for tutoring, and my aunt has a night for tutoring." A working mother described her reliance on a neighbor:

> Now, me being a working parent, my daughter comes home; she's at that age; she's 13, she likes boys. I ask my neighbor, Granny; now she will watch out. I say, "Anybody come to my door, anybody you think is in my house, you go over there and knock on my door."

The extended family also supported children at school

> That boy, he got tons of play cousins and brothers and sisters, so I knew he would always have somebody looking out for him . . . to make sure he didn't get lost . . . that nobody was taking advantage of him.

Community definitions of effective involvement at the school differed from traditionally held notions of parental involvement. Parents advocating for their children as defined by the community involved assertiveness, energy, and a sense of fighting for one's child because the school system could not be trusted to enforce the interests of the least well-served children of color: "Don't wait for the school to call, inquire on your own. Of all the children, they may not remember your own." A parent described her approach: "I'm up front with the teacher, and I'll be in her stuff if she isn't doing what she should be, but she knows that I'll be in baby's stuff if she ain't doing what she's supposed to. Both of them demand respect, and I just let everyone know that I'm up front." Another parent gave this advice: "You have to be in the schools. You have to question things that don't look right. You have to question, question, question, and then you go back home and write it down and question it again."

Based on parents' intentional priorities, they made decisions not to attend certain formalized activities at the school. One parent called PTA "foo-foo" and explained, "You know, I mentioned the jobs. Well, that makes it hard . . . I don't have all afternoon to bake cookies, make spaghetti, and lounge around the school skinnin' and grinnin' in folks' face. Yeah, it sounds great, but food on the table sounds better." According to another parent, "Unless it's a conference, I cannot go to a PTA meeting." A third parent identified higher priorities: "She (the child) needs a spiritual foundation in her life at this point of being a teenager, so we do attend different activities at church on Wednesday night, and especially if things are going on at the school, I just won't be able to make it because of priorities."

Community definitions of effective parental involvement tended to focus on involvement at home, contributions that are largely unrecognized and undervalued by society. Due to the lack of congruence between the home and school cultures, parents must infuse and reinforce middle-class norms of school culture: "We should already have told them the rules and the games. Well, it's not games to play on people, but you know, things that is gonna help them in handling it."

Community families did not see the transition to middle school as a time to relinquish parental guidance; instead they practiced and may in fact have increased assertive, proactive monitoring of both schoolwork and social life: "Stay ahead of them. If they say there is no homework, then where are the books? Where are the books from your locker? There is always homework. You have to stay ahead of them." Parents saw reciprocal links between schoolwork and social life: "I like to see them reading, in the kitchen, anything that might keep them from getting lazy, with the wrong crowd." Another parent expressed her worries about the peer pressure from the streets:

> He ain't really have no trouble, but he did get a really big bunch of rowdy boys that I didn't too much like . . . and I thought that might be a problem, mostly because they were real fast, and I didn't too much know they parents, and they had a lotta free time, they could do more, in terms of running the street than my boy could, so he wanted to be with them all the time. He (my boy) don't have time to be running with no wild neighborhood boys . . . I feel nervous when he starts getting around a bunch of roguish boys.

Families proactively monitored for changes in behavior: "I think she's gotten too big for her britches . . . lotta mouth, body language has changed . . . if I could tell you how many times I tell her, 'you can roll 'em, you can stroll 'em, but you best control 'em'."

One of the activities strongly endorsed by parents both at home and at the school was active cheerleading for their child. At home, families employed active cheerleading because they perceived negative outside influences on self-esteem affecting both academic efforts and social adjustment. These influences could be subtle attacks on personality or devastating blows to self-esteem. One parent worried about the changes in her daughter:

> Up until this point, she was really happy just being herself. But sometimes being yourself is not what others will accept. She really liked bright colors and mixing patterns and things. All of a sudden, my child goes from wearing beautiful socks, to all plain white, which I thought was just tragic.

A parent concerned about her child's adjustment to 6th grade focused on esteem issues: "Because a child has come to school and has to hear, just because they may not be as light as another student and they are put down because they might be large, that shoots a child's self-esteem real low." In response to these pressures, parents encouraged their children at home: "I just want her to be smart. I want her to be the smartest one in her class no matter what, college, whatever." One parent described her approach at home:

> You know how to encourage babies? Clap for them, babble on and on about how good they're doing . . . continually talk to them, show them how to do new things, spend time with them . . . whatever it takes to give them some attention. That shouldn't stop once they're out of Pampers and spending all day with a teacher.

Active cheerleading extended to the school premises:

> Sure, it might not be the biggest deal to you, but if it means something to him, ...well you'd best drag your butt up there and ooh and ah. Not that I'm not interested in what my kids are doing at school, but you have to sometimes go over and beyond a normal response to show them that you are interested, fascinated even.

Parents saw public cheerleading as effective in encouraging their children: "When she was first starting school. . . . I would try to go out and I was really excited about her work and stuff and she was glad that I went."

Community-generated Solutions

In addition to endorsing existing activities and programs which they found beneficial (after-school programs, performance programs, teacher tutoring), families made both general and specific suggestions for further solutions. Some of these centered around programs generated by the community and aimed at specific issues impacting their children. In response to self-esteem problems faced by African American girls, one parent suggested that:

there needs to be something done for African American girls, and I think there needs to be a separate kind of talk about how they adjust to their new body changes, their new surroundings. I think they grow up in a culture where there is an Anglo-Saxon standard of beauty, and so they are at the age where they are going through this adolescent thing, and it seems to me that there is a tide that turns in terms of how comfortable they feel with themselves.

Another parent whose daughter struggled socially said, "There should be something dealing with self-esteem, better open communication among students." A grandparent endorsed the Be Present program for African American girls and their mothers: "One of the things that helped her (granddaughter) is that we are in an organization, called Be Present, that teaches women and girls how to build a support system." Suggestions often centered around drawing on the extended resources of the community in taking direct action to help their children:

> Here is a time when we lose students in the middle schools. We have no one to lose . . . I would give them their marching orders . . . I think that if we held out more challenges to them that "don't let me down," they will live up to that if they knew somebody was watching. They might need a mentoring system where you had three or four or five kids that could talk to one kid about what's going on.

When asked how to get parents involved, one respondent summarized the community feeling that they had solutions to offer: "They (the school) need to have them (the parents) come over and see how the program works with sixth graders and ask *them* what *they* think should be done." Another solution suggested by families was further access to resources. Parents indicated that while resources are not hidden, they are often not presented proactively as tailored to the specific needs of specific children. Parents who became involved on the school premises became aware of these resources.

> So I am saying there are resources here, but I am convinced that because I don't know that they are just pushed at you, but I believe that because I was here and I asked questions and I explored all of the potential resources that could benefit her, that was what made a difference for her in the transition.

Parents who had made the step into involvement on the school grounds expressed strong feelings of efficacy. They felt that they had exerted their rights.

> I like to think that my so-called parent involvement sends up red flags to everyone involved, my girls, the school staff, that I'm an interested parent, a support factor. . . . As a parent you belong in the schools. That's your right. Don't let some teacher who has a tough day get to you with a bad attitude. You don't let stuff like that stop you when you go to the bank, do you?

Families realized that schools often perceived them negatively, and that their presence might be needed to change these perceptions: "We need to let the school know that we love our kids, and we are concerned about their situation."

Such parents experienced positive reinforcement for their actions and readily encouraged others to become similarly involved:

> When they see you come into the schools more, recognizing you, they begin to look up to you a little better and work a little hard for you.... I used to just sit at home.... Now I got to (go to the school) because if I don't, my child is going to lose out as far as getting her education. Start getting involved with the teachers. You begin to see a change.

Some parents recalled extremely rewarding experiences as a result of their on-site presence.

> They called and called. I said, "What is the problem? Is he doing bad?" They said, "No, you just need to come up to the school for the conference." I said, "Oh, Lord, T. done something." So I went up there and Mr. S., he said, "I am so proud of T." And I wanted to cry... because him and this man had a hard time... I said, "That's why y'all kept calling me?" He said, "Yes, we just wanted you to come here so we could see your face," and I said, "Thank you, Jesus!"

One participant described her positive experience: "If you go and meet with the teachers and communicate with them, you can tell a difference. They feel happy, and so do you." There was a positive reciprocal effect of parent involvement: "I've been trying to do more to be involved. And I can see the change ... in the teachers, my son, and how I feel about myself too."

Discussion

These findings help illuminate previous research on family involvement. In particular, issues of capacity and willingness (Fantuzzo et al., 1995), role, efficacy, and invitation (Davies, 1993; Hoover-Dempsey & Sandler, 1997), level of involvement (Epstein, 1995), and community support (Chavkin, 1993; Rich, 1993) may now be viewed through the lens of "invisible families." This investigation extends previous research because when parents didn't show up for interviews, PTA meetings, conferences, and so forth, we went to them, demonstrating our persistence and ingenuity in connecting to the missing parents (Fantuzzo et al., 1995). These parents were marginalized because of race and/or class and not visible at school, labeled as ineffectual, uninvolved, apathetic caretakers who didn't value education (Davies, 1993; McAdoo, 1981), and sometimes described as the bane of conscientious teachers (Meyers & Dowdy, 1998). It is noteworthy that even under these trying circumstances, this sample of parents was able to identify barriers to involvement, conceptualize and implement a community-based framework of involvement, and generate pragmatic solutions to promote family participation in schools. It is time we listen; they have much to tell us.

Families were realistic and self-effacing about their own abilities and those of their neighbors. For example, commonly suggested reasons for lack of involvement were not extensively mentioned by the parents themselves (e.g., low status, aversive school experiences) (Davies, 1993; Fine, 1993). Instead they focused their parenting efforts on self-identified priorities such as church (McGrath & Kuriloff, 1999). They told us that in the face of so many societal deficits and stereotypes (e.g., poor, African-American children can't achieve) they became cheerleaders for their children, bolstering their efforts and self-esteem and assertively monitoring behavior (e.g. to prevent gang membership). This characteristic of their parenting is, perhaps, a response to the environmental challenges their children face.

They told us that in order to provide the academic background they themselves lack, there is an underground network, or extended community family, largely disconnected from the school (Lareau, 1989; McAdoo, 1981; McGrath & Kuriloff, 1999). This collective voice has the potential to ameliorate ineffective parenting and provide leverage to typically disenfranchised parents by sharing parental responsibilities through tutoring, influencing parenting behaviors, and "adopting" the children of ineffectual parents. When these families did approach the school, they did so with an intense advocacy for their children whom they feared would be overlooked by the system. These visits can be reinforcing if educators respect and validate families' efforts. Additionally, families welcomed self-help programs such as parenting training, curriculum tutoring and help with navigating homework. By reassuring parents of their efficacy and genuinely welcoming their input, schools can reduce defensiveness and empower parents. In their own words, families have told us they are, can be, and will continue to be involved. Future research is needed to learn more about the parents who were described by this sample of caregivers as ineffective and about the dynamics of the give and take of the community-family network. What can schools learn from this reciprocity and advocacy? While the "missing voices" parents expressed an interest in tutoring their children, they don't all have the skills necessary to do so. Because of the status of the community-family network, it may be essential for the network to design and deliver training rather than offer conventional tutoring programs that originate from the school. Can schools relinquish their power by supporting a community-based and community-initiated tutoring intervention? This is just one example of the ways in which schools could be effective in recognizing the achievements of these families and establishing collaborative relationships with these active community networks.

An interesting phenomenon that emerged from this study is the presence of community spokespeople. These articulate African American parents negotiated the school culture more easily than other community parents and became advocates of the extended family of the village. As spokespeople, they expressed views and concerns of other least well-served families and children. We need to revisit these families and determine how they can help to connect school personnel with the previously unknown "missing voices" families who were interviewed in this research and the parents whom some participants perceived to be ineffective.

We began this project because three schools expressed concern about the lack of family involvement. One of the middle-school parents we interviewed said: "We're crying out for help and nobody hears us." This mother's plea should give the schools pause. Perhaps, in addition to the problem of finding missing voices, there is also the challenge of listening to the voices that are trying to be heard. Research and intervention efforts that mobilize the community parenting network begun at the elementary school level will continue to scaffold and empower parents as they move with their children to middle school.

References

Armento, B., & Henderson, S. (1999). *Promoting parental involvement in middle school*. Research Atlanta, Inc./ School of Policy Studies Georgia State University, Atlanta, Georgia.

Baker, D. P., & Stevenson, D. L. (1986). Mothers' strategies for children's school achievement: Managing the transition to high school. *Sociology of Education, 59,* 156-166.

Becker, H.J. & Epstein, J.L. (1982). Parent involvement: A study of teacher practices. *Elementary School Journal, 83,* 85-102.

Blyth, D., Simmons, R, & Bush, D. (1978). The transition into early adolescence: A longitudinal comparison of youth in two educational contexts. *Sociology of Education, 51,* 149-162.

Bronfenbrenner, U. (1979). *The ecology of human development: Experiments by nature and design.* Cambridge: Harvard University Press.

Chavkin, N.F. (1993). School social workers helping multiethnic families, schools, and communities join forces. In N.F. Chavkin (Ed.), *Families and schools in a pluralistic society* (pp. 217-225). Albany, NY: SUNY Press.

Christenson, S. L., Rounds, T., & Gorney, D. (1992). Family factors and student achievement: An avenue to increase students' success. *School Psychology Quarterly, 7,* 178-206.

Clark, R. (1983), *Family life and school achievement: Why poor black children succeed or fail.* Chicago, IL: University of Chicago Press.

Comer, J.P. (1984). Home-school relationships as they affect the academic success of children. *Education and Urban Society, 16,* 323-337.

Dauber, S.L. & Epstein, J.L. (1993). Parents' attitudes and practices of involvement in inner-city elementary and middle schools. In N.F. Chavkin (Ed.), *Families and schools in a pluralistic society.* (pp 205-215). Albany, NY: SUNY Press.

Davies, D. (1993). Benefits and barriers to parent involvement: from Portugal to Boston to Liverpool. In N.F. Chavkin (Ed.), *Families and schools in a pluralistic society.* (pp 205-215). Albany, NY: SUNY Press.

Elias, M. J., Clabby, J., Corr, D., Ubriaco, M., & Schuyler, T. (1982). *The improving social awareness-social problem solving project: A case study in school-based action research* (Action Research Workshop Report No. 4) New York: William T. Grant Foundation.

Elias, M. J., Gara, M., Ubriaco, M., Rothbaum, P., Clabby, J., & Schuyler, T. (1986). Impact of a prevention social problem solving intervention on children's coping with middle school stressors. *American Journal of Community Psychology, 14,* 259-275.

Epstein, J.L. (1995). Perspectives and previews on research and policy for school, family, and community partnerships. In A. Booth, & J. Dunn (Eds.), *Family-school links: How do they affect educational outcomes?* New Jersey: Hillsdale.

Epstein, J.L. & Becker, H.J. (1982). Teachers' reported practices of parent involvement: Problems and possibilities. *Elementary School Journal, 83* (2), 103-113.

Epstein, J.L., & Dauber, S. L. (1991). School programs and teacher practices of parent involvement in inner city elementary and middle schools. *Elementary School Journal, 91,* 289-305.

Fantuzzo, J., Davis, G., & Ginsburg, M. D. (1995). Effects of parent involvement in isolation or in combination with peer tutoring on student self-concept and mathematics achievement. *Journal of Educational Psychology, 87* (2), 272-281.

Fantuzzo, J., King J., & Heller, L. (1992). Effects of reciprocal peer tutoring on mathematics and school adjustment: A component analysis. *Journal of Educational Psychology, 84,* 331-339.

Felner, R., & Adan, A. (1988). The school transitional environment project. In R. H. Price, E. L. Cowen, R. P. Lorion, J. Ramos-McKay, & B. Hitchins (Eds.), *Fourteen ounces of prevention: A casebook of exemplary primary prevention programs.* Washington, D.C.: American Psychological Association.

Felner, R., Brand, S., Adam, A., Mulhal, P., Flowers, N., Sartain, B., & DuBois, D. (1993). Restructuring the ecology of the school as an approach to prevention during school transitions: Longitudinal follow-ups and extensions of the School Transitional Environment Project (STEP). *Prevention in Human Services, 10* (2), 103-136.

Felner, R. D., Farber, S. S., & Primavera, J. (1980). Children of divorce, stressful life events, and transitions: A framework for preventative efforts. In R. H. Price, R. F. Ketterer, B. C. Bader, & J. Monahan (Eds.), *Prevention in mental health: Research, policy, and practice* (pp. 87-108). Beverly Hills, CA: Sage.

Fine, M. (1993). [Ap]parent involvement: Reflections on parents, power and urban public schools. *Teacher's College Record, 94,* 682-710.

Green, R. W., & Ollendick, T. H. (1993). Evaluation of a multidimensional program for sixth graders in transition from elementary to middle school. *Journal of Community Psychology, 21,* 162-176.

Hellem, D. W. (1990). Sixth grade transition groups: An approach to primary prevention. *Journal of Primary Prevention, 10* (4), 303-311.

Henry, M.E. (1996). *Parent-school collaboration: Feminist organizational structures and school leadership.* Albany, NY: SUNY Press.

Hoover-Dempsey, K.V., Bassler, O.C., & Brissie, J.S. (1987). Parent involvement: Contributions of teacher efficacy, school SES and other characteristics. *American Educational Research Journal, 24,* 417-435.

Hoover-Dempsey, K.V., Bassler, O.C., & Brissie, J.S. (1992). Explorations in parent-school relations. *Journal of Educational Research, 85,* 287-294.

Hoover-Dempsey, K.V., & Sandler, H.M. (1997). Why do parents become involved in their children's education? *Review of Educational Research, 67,* 3-42.

Lareau, A. (1989). *Home Advantage: Social class and parental intervention in elementary education.* Philadelphia: Falmer Press.

Leonard, C.P., & Elias, M.J. (1993). Entry into middle school: Student factors predicting adaptation to an ecological transition. *Prevention and School Training, 10* (2), 39-57.

Lincoln, Y., & Guba, E. (1985). *Naturalistic Inquiry.* Newbury Park, CA: SAGE Publications, Inc.

McAdoo, H. (1981). *Black Families.* Beverly Hills, CA: Sage Publications.

McCaleb, S.P. (1994). Building a community of learners: A collaboration among teachers, students, families and community. Mahwah, NJ: Erlbaum.

McGrath, D. J. & Kuriloff, P. (1999). "They're going to take the doors off this place.": Upper middle-class parent-school involvement and the educational opportunity of other people's children. *Educational Policy, 13* (5), 603-629.

Menacker, J., Hurwitz, E., & Weldon, W. (1988). Parent-teacher cooperation in schools serving the urban poor. *The Clearing House.* 62. 108-112.

Meyers, B., & Dowdy, J. (1998). *Needs assessment summary.* Submitted as a part of the annual report to the Annenberg Foundation from the Urban Atlanta Coalition Compact.

Meyers, J., Forsbach, T., Finnegan, L., Truscott, S., Gelzheiser, L., & Meyers, B. (April, 1996). *Do parents have a voice in school reform? An empirical investigation of the involvement of parents and other community members in shared decision making.* Presented at the Annual Meetings of the American Educational Research Association. New York, N.Y.

Moles, O.C. (1993). Collaboration between schools and disadvantaged parents: Obstacles and opening. In N.F. Chavkin (Ed.), *Families and schools in a pluralistic society* (pp. 21-49). Albany, NY: SUNY Press.

National Association of Secondary School Principals (1993). Washington D.C.: Author.

National Commission on Children. (1991). *Speaking of kids: A national survey of children and parents.* Washington, DC: Author.

Parkes, C.M. (1971). Psycho-social transitions: A field of study. *Social Science and Medicine, 5,* 101-115.

Raffaele, L., & Knoff, H. (1999). Improving home-school collaboration with disadvantaged families: Organizational principles, perspectives and approaches. *School Psychology Review, 28* (3), 448-466.

Rich, D. (1993). Building the bridge to reach minority parents: education infrastructure supporting success for all children. In N.F. Chavkin (Ed.), Families and schools in a pluralistic society (pp.235-243). Albany, N.Y.: SUNY Press.

Rutherford, B., & Billig, S. (1995). Eight lessons of parent, family, and community involvement in the middle grades. *Phi Delta Kappan, 77* (1), 64-66.

Slaughter-Defoe, D.T. (1991). Parental educational choice: Some African American dilemmas. *Journal of Negro Education, 60* (3) 354-360.

Slaughter, D.T. & Kuehne, V.S. (1988). Improving Black education: Perspectives on parent involvement. *Urban League Review,* 59-75.

Spradley, J.P. (1979). *The ethnographic interview.* New York: Holt, Rinehart, & Winston.

Strauss, A., & Corbin, J. (1990). *Basics of qualitative research: Grounded theory procedures and techniques.* Newbury Park, CA: SAGE Publications, Inc.

Walker, E.V.S. (1993) Caswell County Training School, 1933-1969: Relationships between community and school. *Harvard Educational Review, 63* (2) 161-182.

Wentzel, K.R. (1998). Social relationships and motivation in middle school: The role of parents, teachers and peers. *Journal of Educational Psychology, 90* (2), 202-209.

Chapter 7
Joanne Kilgour Dowdy
with Martha Abbott-Shim,
Lynn Briggs, Florence Hardney-Hinds,
and Tracy Woodhall

Poetry in the Middle School Classroom

An Artist/Activist and Teacher Collaboration Leading to Reform

I am an activist teacher/artist/student. These multiple roles come to me naturally because I claim my heritage from the order of Black women artist/activist/educators who include Mary Mc Leod Bethune, Frances Ellen Watkins Harper, Fannie Barrier Williams, Anna Julia Cooper, Fannie Jackson Coppin, Sarah J. Early, and Hallie Q. Brown (Robinson, 2001). The acknowledgment of my ancestors came to me while I was working as a University Fellow in the Urban Atlanta Coalition Compact (1997–2001). After the first year of the Urban Atlanta Coalition Compact's reform initiative in Middle School, the name I have chosen for the school in this story, I became aware of the importance of my role as the "inspector." I invented this label for myself after realizing that my arrival at the school was a signal to the staff and teachers of the school that those children "least well-served"[1] were my wards. I was also put in the position of ensuring that the teachers in the school were aware of their responsibility to me when it came to creating an environment that was supportive of these African-American children's success.

The Black female community activists who founded schools in the late nineteenth and twentieth centuries saw their commitment to the education of women as the means to improve the condition of all Blacks. Their shared philosophy was based on three tenets: (a) the moral superiority of women, (b) the view that the Black woman was entirely responsible for the development of all Blacks, and (c) the expectation that Black women would attend to the needs of their (Black) sisters (Perkins, 1980). Publications such as Anna Julia Cooper's book *A Voice from the South* (1892) in which she wrote on womanhood and presentations of hers in 1899 (at the Hampton Negro Conference) are testimonials to the concern that Black educated women expressed at the time regarding moral development in girls and women in their urban American communities.

The "club women" were important to the transformation of the image of Black women after abolition in 1865. These club women, as the progressive Black women have been referred to, were determined to erase the stereotype of Black women as licentious because of their historic subjugation to White slave masters (Batker, 1998). Giddings (1984) also describes the development of the "cult of true womanhood" as it was translated from the White community by Black club women who worked to change the material and moral conditions of the newly freed Black community postslavery. Mary Mc Leod Bethune, an educator and activist, claimed that Black women "recognized the importance of uplifting [their] people through social, civic, and religious activities" (Lerner, 1973). Mary Church Terrell, educator and writer, declared the war on immorality and low socio-economic status among Blacks by insisting that the more intelligent and influential Blacks had a responsibility to "uplift those beneath them" (Higginbotham, 1993, p. 206). Nannie Burroughs, school principal and activist, spoke and wrote about the "respectability" of the working-class woman, encouraging club women who were involved in social uplift programs to find the "ordinary, common-sense, spirit filled everyday woman" and involve her in the movement for racial uplift (Higginbotham, 1993, p. 208).

The advent of the abolition of slavery led to a demand for improved educational resources. It was in this national environment of "re-visioning" the future of Black people that the women leaders began organizing schools that gave children the kind of experiences that enabled them to go beyond menial tasks. Reading, writing, and arithmetic were foundation courses for all Blacks enrolled as beginning students, regardless of age and former experience. These club women displayed through their actions a formidable faith in the potential of Blacks and the promising future that awaited them and the nation. Through their role as activists, these community leaders were able to mobilize forces that transformed the post-slavery population. In their commitment to improving the lot of the Black masses, they exhibited the determination of their forbears to outlive the stigma associated with slavery and the legacy of compromised opportunities for African descendants. Activism in the work of this gathering of sisters represented a militant attitude against the opposing forces of racism, sexism, and classism.

The Urban Atlanta Coalition Compact

In the tradition of the club women of the post-slavery era, the Urban Atlanta Coalition Compact was created to serve the least successful African American students in the public schools of metropolitan Atlanta. The UACC (Urban Atlanta Coalition Compact) served seven schools from 1997 to 2001. At each of these schools a university fellow (UF) was the contact person between the university and the school. The fellow's duties included creating a school profile based on interviews with a broad representation of teachers, students, faculty, support staff, and parents. The UF also facilitated communication between the director of the UACC and the leaders of the action team, a school-based teacher group. The goal here was to relay information efficiently from the individual school to the university as planning for school activities and other UACC business was conducted. The UF was also expected to work in individual classrooms as the need for her expertise arose. As a Language Arts specialist I was expected to provide classroom support for the faculty in that unit. The UF worked with the Action Team to promote the implementation of the reform initiatives that had been created to improve the education of the least well-served African American students in the school (Obidah, 1999).

In my role as university fellow at Middle School, the only middle school in the Urban Atlanta Coalition Compact, I implemented several of the features for successful involvement with the faculty and students. These benchmarks are described in Delpit's "Ten Factors Essential to Success in Urban Classrooms" (personal communication, 1998) (See Table 1).

In one eighth grade classroom in Middle School, part of a small city school system in northeast Georgia, the university fellow and a group of teachers from the language arts faculty implemented a drama initiative in the Language Arts classroom. This project

TABLE 1. Ten Factors Essential to Success in Urban Classrooms

1. Do not teach less content to poor, urban children, but understand their brilliance and teach more!
2. Whatever methodology or instructional program is used, demand critical thinking.
3. Assure that all children gain access to "basic skills," the conventions and strategies that are essential to success in American education.
4. Provide the emotional ego strength to challenge racist societal views of the competence and worthiness of the children and their families.
5. Recognize and build on strengths.
6. Use familiar metaphors and experiences from the children's world to connect what they already know to school knowledge.
7. Create a sense of family and caring.
8. Monitor and assess needs and then address them with a wealth of diverse strategies.
9. Honor and respect the children's home culture(s).
10. Foster a sense of children's connection to community to something greater than themselves.

developed into a nine-week unit of drama exercises and writing activities that supported the development of the writing skills of the low-achieving students in two classes. In two other classes we introduced a unit where students worked to collect and translate the slang terms and idioms from their home language, Black English, into standard English versions. The point of the exercise was to first open a space in the classroom where students felt free to bring in their home language and celebrate it. Then, second, to build a bridge to standard English so that they could feel comfortable going back and forth from one form of the language to another, enriched by the knowledge that they had more than one mode of communication available to them (Baker, 2002). The Action Team also supported a plan for training teachers in anti-racism techniques and an individualized academic program for students who had been retained at Middle School in the year that the UACC reform initiative arrived at the school.

Middle School represented a microcosm of the city in which it was situated. Even though 80 percent of the teachers and staff at Middle School voted to become involved with the UACC, I still feel that my presence in the school generated a watchful attitude among the faculty. This perceived reservation among the faculty had a great impact on my feeling of being a club woman of the nineteenth century. My job description led me to ask questions about the students who were not on grade level in reading and writing, which led me to situations that pitted my sense of moral responsibility and responsibility as a UF against the "conventions" of the White-dominated parent association. The high percentage of children from the lower economic neighborhoods and the way in which the school faculty were developing measures to ensure the success of the failing African Americans in their charge were only two of the hot issues that I had to negotiate over the first year.

In the presence of a powerful professional parent group it was difficult to feel comfortable in the school. My feeling of being an "interrupter" of the school culture or "inspector" of the premises where Black children were being educated according to White middle-class values (Delpit, 1995), can best be explained through some of the comments that I documented during the initial self-study that the school did in 1998. The quotes from teachers, parents, and staff members that stand out to me after three years include: "Even though this [Black] kid may have a 'B' average and the White kid has a 'B' average, more time is spent with the White one" (staff); and "there are [teachers] who are victims of their training and they think that the issue with the African American child is impenetrable" (parent). From the staff I heard: "Looks like almost two schools, White school here, black school there;" and there was a "lack of understanding of the different cultures that we have here, primarily lack of understanding between the Black and White culture." The strongest comment came from a mother who had claimed that the school should not "discount [her] as a Black parent ['cause] I'm just as concerned about my child. I will not allow [them] to bring down . . . his self-esteem."

Middle School

Middle School is part of a small city school cluster. There are seven elementary schools, one middle school, and one high school in this urban environment. The elementary schools have traditionally housed populations of children of the same racial background. When the students arrive at Middle School, it is, for most, the first time that they encounter children of a different racial background in their classroom learning environment. There is also a wide range in the economic levels of the children from the Black and White majority neighborhoods. These differences in racial and economic status provide an undercurrent of tension in the school. However, interviews with Black and White students conducted by a research team (Meyers, Dowdy, & Paterson, 2000) revealed the many instances where teachers of both races gave unstintingly to the Black children who graduated to Middle School from a predominantly Black elementary school.

The school's demographics represent the composition of the city in which the children live. Middle School has 622 students of which 55% are Black, 41% are White, 1% are Hispanic, and 3% are multiracial and international, and 39% are eligible for free/reduced lunches (Georgia Public Education Report Card, 1999–2000). The divide between the social backgrounds of the Black and White children may be partly explained by the fact that many of the Black children live in public housing while the White children live in middle-class homes. Both of these groups live within easy reach of the school and can be seen walking, cycling, traveling in school buses, or being driven by their parents and guardians.

In my role as university fellow I had worked on the school reform project (UACC) at Middle School for three years (starting 1997) before the arts integration project was launched in March 2001. The teachers who were interested in doing drama early on in the reform project were in the Language Arts classrooms. They formed a small "study group" and began meeting off-hours in order to try out exercises that they would later do in their classrooms. This kinesthetic approach to teaching (Dowdy, 1999) became an opportunity to see teachers from another perspective. They were not only interested in the students succeeding in the traditional curriculum but also wanted to see their charges come in to their own and be proud of their heritage as Black people with a history of success in the sciences and arts. These teachers were activists in their own right. They claimed the space of the acting workshop to hone their skills at improving the chances of reaching the students not being served by the traditional classroom pedagogy. Later on, I also got a chance to observe students who were successful at learning by doing and began to understand the ways in which staff development in the use of the arts for instruction could change teachers for the better and enhance the success of the students.

In the third year of my work with the teachers, staff, and pupils at Middle School, I was invited to design and conduct a series of workshops for the Language Arts faculty.

The teachers from the language arts faculty completed a series of four workshops, including "Learning by Moving: Poetry in the Classroom" (Dowdy, 1999). Among the items that we played with during that session were my film frame/acting/writing exercise as described in the steps that follow. A favorite poem among the teachers was "My Mother's Hands" (author unknown):

> Such beautiful, beautiful hands!
>   They're neither white nor small;
> And you, I know, would scarcely think
>   That they are fair at all.
> I've looked on hands whose form and hue
>   A sculptor's dream might be;
> Yet are those aged, wrinkled hands
>   More beautiful to me.
>
> Such beautiful, beautiful hands!
>   Though heart were weary and sad,
> Those patient hands kept toiling on,
>   That the children might be glad.
> I always weep, as, looking back
>   To childhood's distant day,
> I think how those hands rested not
>   When mine were at their play.
>
> Such beautiful, beautiful hands!
>   They're growing feeble now,
> For time and pain have left their mark
>   On hands and heart and brow.
> Alas! Alas! The nearing time,
>   And the sad, sad day to me,
> When 'neath the daisies, out of sight,
>   These hands will folded be.
>
> But on! This shadow-land,
>   Where all is bright and fair,
> I know full well these dear old hands
>   Will palms of victory bear;
> Where crystal streams through endless years
>   Flow over golden sands,
> And where the old grow young again,
>   I'll clasp my mother's hands.

In the workshop I encouraged the group of five or six teachers to read poems like this one, drawing the stories, creating biographies about the lead characters in the poems they selected to work on, and writing editorials/songs/new poems/letters based on the characters described in the poems. I also asked the teachers in the workshop to consider what they would do with the poetry workshop in their classrooms and discuss ideas about how I could facilitate their success.

The Philosophy Behind the Language Arts Unit

The teachers in the Language Arts faculty needed to learn new methods of poetry instruction. "We [teachers] have to do all the things in the book, we aren't taught to help students see the characters in the poem and to think about how these people feel when they say the lines in the poem," was one lament. We, the teachers involved in the Language Arts study group and myself, were discussing ways to engage students during a workshop session organized by the Peachtree Urban Writing Project. Right then I knew that I had to change the preparation for teaching poetry in Middle School. The opportunity to work through some of the activities that could be included in a poetry workshop became available through the Atlanta Partnership for Arts in Learning (APAL) initiative (funded in part by Fonda Foundation in 2001). In collaboration with three teachers in the school, I developed a series of lessons that helped students explore poetry from an actor's perspective. The steps would lead them to identify the character in a poem and then to demonstrate their understanding of the character through the performance of the poem.

Since I believe, along with others, that we all participate in play-acting from early childhood well into our mature years (Lederer, 1981), I worked to create an environment that was highly responsive to experiments. Coaxing people to act "as if" allows them the opportunity to reveal their feelings, to commit to the project at hand, and to experience the support of a group as they develop their creative responses to a poem (King, 1981). With these ideas in mind, I provided choices of poetry from authors Langston Hughes, Marge Piercy, Beah Richards, Paul Laurence Dunbar, Jaki Shelton Green, Nikki Giovanni, and Walt Whitman. These selections from various poets give students, whether teachers or young people, a chance to find their own level of engagement (i.e., the kind of issues they are willing to "act out" in public). The topics in my poetry collection include friendship, loneliness, racism, domestic abuse, women's rights, parents and children, and love. The wide range of poems collected from books, former students, email messages, newspapers, journals, and newsletters allowed each participant the chance to find texts that fit his or her mood, experience, and interest.

The poetry workshop gave me an opportunity to "operationalize" the ten factors essential to success in urban classrooms. Dr. Delpit had repeatedly referred to our "marching orders" over the time that we worked in the UACC as the factors which included and were not exclusive to this list of ideas: develop content-rich classes, encourage critical thinking, using "basic skills" as a fact of formal education, allowing students to develop the "ego strength to challenge racist societal views" of their potential, building on strengths, using children's home language of Black English to build a bridge to formal school English, creating a family atmosphere in the school, addressing diverse needs and attending to them with various strategies, honoring the children's home culture, and developing a sense of connectedness to the community (so that children can think of themselves beyond the role of an individual).

I certainly felt that after three years' work in Middle School that the university fellow had to get into the classrooms and make a difference in the individual lives of the students. Teachers had to begin to demonstrate their commitment to the philosophy of high expectations for the least well-served African American students if they were going to move into the last phase of the reform agenda. More importantly, as an acknowledged Black club woman working at the end of the twentieth century, I was impatient to see the children who had been suffering under the restraints of the desk/pencil/paper traditional mode of teaching move over to a experiential and thus more successful way of learning. I knew that the children who learned best by being involved in the lesson, which should have included all the middle school students, were ready for engagement through UACC-inspired teaching. I also felt that the club woman part of myself was impatient to make changes for the sake of the children who were my particular concern.

The Poetry Workshop

At the invitation of the three teachers on the Atlanta Partnership for Arts in Learning (APAL) team Tracy, Lynn, Florence and I met and discussed the topics they were interested in exploring with their grades 6, 7, and 8 classes. At the second meeting, I presented a five-week workshop schedule to the teachers which they agreed to use in their planning of the unit we called "Character Development Through the Study of Text." My workshop plan was designed to dovetail with the work that the teachers were doing on their own in each of the three classrooms selected for the workshop. The outline enhanced their plans for the unit on character development, and it covered the Quality Core Curriculum standards that they were expected to meet in their lessons.

The workshop outline was designed to help us keep on track with the progress of each teacher and the class that she taught. The five-block schedule would also allow me to slip in and out of each teacher's journey easily because I would know what block of the workshop was being addressed during each week that the team worked on the unit. The teachers could use my exercises whenever they were appropriate to the text and the themes that were being developed. I would supplement that process by leading a particular exercise on the day that I visited each class to do "performance" work.

As an arts-based team, we agreed on a list of guidelines at the start of the collaboration. These guidelines included a meeting with each teacher before we did our team presentation/performance activity in each class. I would be presented as a "performer," not a literature teacher, and we would videotape all fifteen classes and review them at the end of the unit. Our first meeting as a team would be videotaped, and we would reflect on it at the end of the semester to see how far we had succeeded in accomplishing our goals. And, we would use clips from our tape recordings to present at national conferences and APAL meetings so we could share our journey in the CD workshop with other artists and teachers. Most importantly, we agreed to be open to change and responsive to the needs of the students in order to shape the poetry unit for their success in discovering character through text study (Team Meetings, April 2001).

The Five Blocks of the Workshop

I presented the following five blocks in my role as artist collaborator to Tracy, Lynn, and Florence, the APAL team, at the first meeting on our Character Development unit.

Week 1: Introduction to the Poetry Workshop
- Students would find poems from the collection in the library and look for clues to the character's voice in the text.
- Teachers would also choose a poem for their own exploration in the workshop.

Week 2: Practice with Poems
Activities would lead students to:
- Identify with the character's voice.
- Decide on the point of the poem; the story line (i.e., beginning, middle, and end); and the attitude of the speaker.
- Write about the story that is being told in the poem.

Week 3: Choosing the Character
- Students will find out about the poet by doing research on the history, geography, and events that are depicted in the poem.
- Students will find a person or community that they can compare to the person/events in the poem.
- Students will interview with someone in the community who reminds them of the character. Write about the way that you identify with the character/community; do improvised scenes in class in character; write as if you were the character (i.e., diary entries, newspaper editorials, letters to loved ones, etc.).

Week 4: Rehearsal of Characters
- Students will role play in couples to develop the voice of the character, i.e., the body language, the dialect, the clothing choices, etc.
- Teachers will put characters in situations and let them improvise their reaction by speaking with someone whom they just met (i.e., on the phone, at the mall, on the street looking for a house they have never seen before).
- Students will write about the experiences that came out of the improvisations based on character and situation.

Week 5: Presentation of the Characters Doing Their Poems
- Students will review the research that led to the final choices (i.e., clothes, voice, dialect, historical perspective) of the character.
- Class looks at videotapes done during the journey to the final choices on character presentations to celebrate the journey.
- Class does a review of interviews done with individuals in the community through scripted scenes that the students created.
- The class will collect written documents from students in the voice of the character (i.e., letters, diary entries, newspaper articles, etc.) that will be shared with other audiences.
- All "totems" that students and teachers produced as representations of their characters (i.e., paintings, new poetry, video presentations, music, or art projects) will be shown in the classrooms.

I also gave the teachers a list of steps for analyzing a poem to support their work while I was out of the classroom. These steps were designed to help the students think independently and to give the teachers some choices in their development of each week's theme. This would ensure that the team did not feel tied to the blocks that were outlined in my workshop plan (see Table 2).

One Teacher's Lesson Plans for the Sixth Grade

My meetings with the three teachers evolved to a point where we shared a mutual language, encouraging the students to see things from the character's point of view. From the first lesson planning event, Tracy, the sixth grade teacher, began using a five-step plan to lead students through the journey that would help them realize the first step in the poetry workshop.

Step 1: Draw on the background of the students. This might be done by referencing the poems that the students read from the collection they looked at the day before. Students would then be encouraged to tell about the stories that their poems represented.

TABLE 2. Steps to Presenting a Poem: A Cheat Sheet for Students and Teachers

1. Read the title.
2. Read the poem.
3. Decide on the story line (i.e., beginning, middle, and end).
4. What is the point of the poem?
5. What is the attitude of the speaker?
6. How do you relate to the attitude of the speaker?
7. Practice reading the poem out loud in the attitude you feel represents the character's feelings.
8. Listen to other people read the poem to you.
9. Write out the poem in your own handwriting.
10. What are some important features of the poem (i.e., repetition, length of the lines, order of the ideas, last word on each line, not sentence)?
11. What points are important in the sequence of the story line (i.e., what happens in order of time/events)?
12. Memorize the poem.
13. Talk the poem as if you were someone else (i.e., your parent or least favorite teacher).
14. Use the poem as an excerpt of a conversation (i.e., pretend you are on the phone with a friend, and you answer a question by using the poem you have memorized).
15. Listen to yourself performing the poem in character on a tape recording/video recording. Make changes to your presentation according to the effect that you are working to achieve.
16. Decide on the reason you need to say the poem (i.e., to convince, annoy, anger, show resentment, or insult someone).
17. Decide on an event in your life that makes you feel like the character you are representing. How do you relate to the situation being represented in the poem?
18. Reflect on the specific event, or others like it before you present the poem each time. This exercise will help you to concentrate and present the poem in a convincing manner.
19. Reflect on your original take on the poem. How has it changed since you completed these steps on the list above? How has it remained the same?
20. Enjoy sharing the poem in character with others!

Step 2: We can get the students to focus on the attitudes/needs of each character by playing two games.

Game 1: Pack a bag with objects that you believe your character would take on a journey (i.e., list the items, imagine the pieces, and draw them or prepare to tell your partner what things your character has in the bag and why they are there (Kaufman, 1999).

Game 2: Play Statues—each student should find a physical shape to stand/sit/lie in that represents the attitude of the character (e.g., sad, angry, happy, expectant). Take Polaroid pictures of the students in their poses and then hang them on a wall for the viewing of the whole class. Students will be encouraged to pick one of the poses that is different from their own character's body shape and to draw it—even stick figures or three-dimensional models are acceptable. Students should also have to talk to each other while holding the pose of their statue. This means that they have to adjust their voices and comments to match the physical reality of the statue (e.g., a sad pose produces a sad voice with many despondent comments about the topic that was presented to the character).

Step 3: Students should experiment with their poems in different physical/vocal attitudes. This will help them realize the point of the poem and the possible ways in which the poet could be supported in making the story line clear. By showing how the character feels when he/she presents the lines in the poem, students should have a chance to step outside their normal way of speaking and thinking (e.g., speaking in an excited voice or a slow, depressed tone).

Step 4: Students should be encouraged to write about the story that is presented in their poem. The story could be told in another form (e.g., in the form of a letter, a newspaper editorial, an advertisement, or a song). Each of these forms of the original story line presented in the poem should make the same point as the one made in the original poem. The students should also be encouraged to share their new form of the story with the rest of the class in their character's voice.

Tracy's development of the four-step lesson plan provided a very useful tool for the other teachers and myself. We began to talk in terms of steps and what we thought should happen at each point in the workshop class. The idea of scaffolding the workshop classes in steps allowed Tracy and the other teachers to feel safe within the creative environment. Because they did not consider themselves "artists," they needed the safety of the traditional language of lesson planning so that they could at least begin a class with an idea of what might take place in that session. If the class developed in a way that was unexpected, for example, a student were to create a character faster than the others, then Tracy could point that individual to another step to further his or her creativity. In other words, the steps acted as a safety net for the teachers. The safety net was a way of thinking about the class and how to facilitate student learning within each session.

We came to understand the process of each class as a series of steps. Tracy's idea was that each child should (a) show that he or she understands key concepts, such as a characters' attitudes and actions, that we were teaching on the given day; (b) see the concept made personal through a demonstration, i.e., they could play statues and learn about physicalization; (c) choose a vehicle (e.g., play a game like statues), that gave the students practical experience with the concept so that the teachers and myself could see them play and commit to the emotional reality of the situation that the game demanded of them; (d) have a chance to practice and write about his or her experiences (e.g., play a statue, draw a statue, and then write about what it was like talking as the character of the statue; and (e) begin practicing using the voices of the selected characters (e.g., a character based on Sojourner Truth should exhibit an authoritative voice). These steps allowed the team to think in a sequential manner and to come up with age-appropriate activities for the three grade levels.

Florence chose to ask the eighth grade students to bring in objects that represented their characters. Lynn asked the students in the seventh grade to do a Venn diagram that would help them compare and contrast one character to another. They also compared features of their lives to those that they created for their characters and thereby gained insight into the background of the life that they had imagined for each persona. The conversations that evolved from the activity in the eighth grade would help the students see that they could not do all poems in their own voice/attitude. Instead, they would need to develop a menu of personae with different voices and physical characteristics, so that they could do convincing presentations of their characters.

Lesson Plan for the Rehearsal of Characters

By the fourth week of the workshop, the poetry workshop team had a common language of terms. We began to use such terms as getting in character, motivation for speaking like the character, and body language that creates the impression of the character or physicalization. We found that we could work through a general lesson plan and that it would be adapted to each of the three classrooms. Next we provided the boiler-plate agreed upon at the meeting preceding the rehearsal of the characters in the poem. This is what the four-part lesson plan looked like for the week's first lesson:

Step 1: Warm-up for the exercise on demonstrating the character in the poem
- Generate a list of characters.
- Discuss the people in your life that these characters remind you of.
- Identify one character whom you want to study.
- List the reasons why the character reminds you of that person and why.

Step 2: Show the character in the poem
- Joanne presents her character from the autobiographical work "Between Me and the Lord," written and performed by her (Dowdy et al., 2000).
- Talk about the person who you chose to model your character on.
- Present your poem : The Good Little Girl by A. A. Milne
    This poem, included in my autobiographical work, "Between Me and the Lord," was used to demonstrate some important connections to my early life. Students were encouraged to ask about my life in Trinidad, where I was born, and about the relatives who peopled my early years on the island (Dowdy, 2002).
- Present the bag that the character has and the objects that are packed in it.
- Respond to the questions from the class on the contents.
- Joanne shares pictures of herself in costume as the "good girl."

Step 3: Joint Practice: We discuss the presentation by Joanne with the class
- We want to focus on how they might put it together (e.g., What do they need to do to make the character credible?).
- Students will be invited to write a short description of why those objects are in their bag
- Students will share their descriptions with the class.

Step 4: Interviews in couples: To invite students to talk as their characters based on their research leading up to this interview
- Each person will have 4 minutes to talk in character before he or she switches over to let the other partner speak in character.

Talking in character. Talking in character became the touchstone of the poetry workshop. One student said that it was "very hard" to maintain the attitude of the character, especially if you were doing the exercise on a day when one did not feel like being "happy or sad" or any other mood that the character represented. During the interviews of the characters, students realized that they could not say things that were uninformed or not determined by a logical analysis of a character's background. For example, if they at first indicated that a person was twelve years old and an immigrant, they could not later say in the interview that the person was an American-born teenager who liked listening to Tupac Shakur's music.

Characters in interviews. The "reality test" that the interview situations with characters provided brought home two ideas to the teachers and the students. First, they noted that while the character's reality is based on imagination to some degree, there must be a logic to the way that the imagined reality is organized. In other words, if you want your audience to believe your character, you are responsible for building that credibility on a firm foundation of facts and history woven together into a believable story.

The students became actors in this journey, working through the upper levels of Bloom's taxonomy, particularly analysis and synthesis, as they brought characters to life in the classroom (Bloom, 1971). This integration of arts in learning was the premise of the project. Those students who did not think deeply about their character's autobiography had a difficult time committing their imaginations to the process of the interviews. In contrast, those who invested their imaginations and critical thinking reached a very deep understanding of the concepts in the state's Quality Core Curriculum.

The teachers felt challenged by the exercises that we developed for the class. When observing the teacher presenting her own character and then answering questions about the character's history, hobby, and interests, it became patently clear that she did not expect the students to take the exercise as seriously as they did on that day. Having entered the world of play and the level of concentration that the students brought to the logic of that imaginary space, the teacher had to surrender her control of the situation as a leader and abide by the rules of the game. This was a new and scary experience for the teacher. She talked with me during a planning session about feeling "vulnerable" in front of the students and the fact that she did not think deeply about the way in which the character would draw on her own experience as a child before presenting her work. This was an important piece of the journey for both the teacher and the students because it meant that they were beginning to see the importance of bringing life experience into the classroom (Ladson-Billings, 2002). The least well-served students now had a chance to better use their home experience in the classroom without it being subjected to criticism or being made invisible. It also meant that they could connect with the poet's intentions and the reasons that the lines of the poem were put together in particular ways. The students began to notice the way lines were broken up to create emotional effects when the poem was read and the choice of words that the poets used to create powerful images. It became clear to the workshop participants that the emotional impact of the poem had to be based on the poet's experiences. Their awareness of the poet's investment in the poem's emotional reality encouraged them to commit serious attention to the work of creating dramatic presentations.

On two occasions the other teachers talked about their own difficulty with some of the tasks that they had created for the workshop. Since I encouraged the teaching team to do the series of steps that they were recommending to the students, they sometimes found themselves feeling anxious when they had to present their work to the class. They realized that play acting brought them to a new level of appreciation of the courage of the adolescents who had to stand in front of the class and reveal emotions they were not accustomed to exploring in public. One student chose a poem about suicide and if it were not for his playful nature in the other aspects of the class, I would have taken him very seriously and asked the school counselor to have a talk with him in case he was contemplating some unfortunate action against himself. This student was also able to perform the poem in different moods, convincing us all that he was in control of the character rather than the other way around.

A young woman who was considered a problem by most of her teachers and the administrators of the school took an immense interest in the character behind "Ain't I a Woman," a speech by Sojourner Truth (Painter, 1996). Her teacher, Florence, admitted to me that she had never seen this student commit so much energy to a class assignment. It was also evident that because of the powerful presence of this student and her intense interest in her character's development that the other students in the class took the assignment of learning their poems very seriously. They also played in a focused way so that they discovered traits about their characters that they would not have imagined or allowed themselves to consider by reading the poems and telling their teacher what they thought the poet meant by writing about the character in a particular way.

The students in Florence's class blossomed as they took ownership of their journey to discover the logic behind the stories that each poem represented. One student decided to interview a basketball player on the school team because she believed that this player's personality represented the character in the poem. After her interview, she was able to imitate the player's voice and attitude, using these features to represent the character in her poem. The student showed the class a different side of her personality and impressed them with her ability to observe people and translate her findings into the work of character representation.

Discussion

Poetry allows us to make an emotional connection with the characters represented in the stories that poets create. We may find ourselves relinquishing preconceived notions about another person based on race, class, or socio-economic status because we come to identify with the personality we recognized in the poem. This empathy helps us to cut to the core of the human experience that is rendered through the lines on the page. Adolescents are as vulnerable to the transforming experience as their teachers. The subjects that are addressed in their choice of poetry can give them an opportunity to deal with their feelings and perception of situations in a safe environment. The poetry workshop that we sponsored also invited students to experience the journey of making meaning through different forms of expression (e.g., drawing, acting, music, video presentations) to represent their understanding of the stories and the characters that poems represent.

Multiple ways of knowing. There are many ways of knowing and expressing our experience. Harste (1994) reminds us that different symbol systems, used for communication among human beings, "represent ways humans have learned to mediate the world in an attempt to make and share meaning" (p. 29). It is this incentive to find many ways to express understanding and connection with the journey of human experience that organizes students' efforts to express the levels on which they "hear" the voice of characters. To challenge the classes that we teach, adults or young people need to expand their ways of knowing. Through, for example, drama, art, and language, students are encouraged to increase the growth of levels of understanding in all areas of learning inside and outside the classroom (Short, Harste, and Burke, 1996).

The changes in the ways of knowing and communicating were evident to the teachers. A review of the electronic messages circulated between the teachers and myself is a helpful way to understand how the poetry workshop began to affect the classrooms where we worked for five weeks.

Tracy wrote early on in the workshop:

Today we read "The Black Cat" excerpt . . . we discussed vocabulary, meaning, attitude and the needs of the poet, then I read the poem to them in "different voices" . . . the kids were great, they were telling me . . . "no, no, not like that . . . that's too high a voice, go deeper, sound scarier, sound gruffer . . . do a 'proper' English accent . . . that's too sing songy . . . more anger . . .". We had FUN! . . . they practice their own poems with each other next. This experience is really pushing me to do things differently . . . I'm growing as a teacher because of this.

Lynn was relieved to report that:

> Three boys in my class who have done almost NOTHING all year participated in Wednesday's statue exercise. Even if this doesn't raise anyone's test scores, that's enough for me. I had great success with statues the rest of the day, but I did not do Polaroids on my own. I simply extended the time we spent with statues and had some of the groups do a little performance by rotation through lines of their poems. It was really cool.

It is also important to mention that the teachers began using aspects of their training that they had formerly found neither time and interest nor enthusiasm to bring into the classroom. For example, Tracy found that her experience with drawing could be used to encourage students to sketch characters and reflect on emotions and situations described in the poems. She also brought her fondness of music to the attention of the students when she dramatized her character and talked about the character's background. In her presentation during Week 4 of the workshop, she did her whole character's bag activity to the accompaniment of music. She danced during a part of the presentation, and the students seemed to transform from onlookers to fellow actors before our very eyes. I imagine that it looked to them as though their teacher had suddenly become more "human", less of an authoritative figure who existed solely in order to give them directions—or part of a club that the students granted tremendous respect.

Lynn, a second teacher on the team, was able to focus on her interest on the community politics that were affecting the school system at the time of the project. By insisting that her students go out into the community and talk with people who reminded them of the characters that the poems helped them create, she was making the Language Arts classroom a living experience and demonstrating the usefulness and power of language. The interviews that the students did with parents and professionals in their community not only provided an experience of preparing and performing live interviews but the opportunity to bring that information back so that their peers and teachers could benefit from the research. Mock interviews based on actual conversations with adults outside the classroom gave some students a forum to present themselves as adults with ample experience. They acted like people with personae that were completely different from their daily childhood masks. This transformation elicited a variety of responses from their classmates including surprise, pride, a competitive spirit, and respect for the kind of patience and collaboration that it takes for people to interview others. They also learned to cull the most important pieces of information from the discussion and figure out how to present these to an interested audience.

The reform agenda. Clearly, the expectations that the UACC reform agenda had primed me to have in relation to the student learning and teacher expectations in the classroom were beginning to take concrete form in this workshop. It was no accident that some male students, mostly Black, began to participate in the workshop. Before the workshop they may have felt invisible in the classrooms with the White teachers. They may have had a similar experience to the graduate students who described themselves as "noises in the attic" of the White academic environment of higher education (Dowdy, Givens, Murillo, Shenoy & Villenas, 2000). Or, the students might have identified with Carter Woodson's description of the miseducation of the Negro and what it was like to be illfitted for a productive life in a Eurocentric culture (Woodson, 1994).

But the poetry project made sure that the students were invited to bring their experiences and creativity to the learning situation They were encouraged to participate as artists of equal status with the other students. Delpit's admonitions that the classroom show value for the student's culture and that teachers should use the experiences of students as a bridge to new knowledge were clearly demonstrated in these children's use of their home-community's languages (Delpit, 2002). The fact that each student was encouraged to use his or her home language, Black English, in the journey to describing and performing the characters in the poems created a space for the different cultures to co-exist in Middle School.

Critical thinking was also a necessary part of the journey to performing the poems. The students had to ask questions of the poet, the poem, themselves, and their classmates in order to construct realistic personae for their final project. The ways in which individual learners showed their life experiences and needs as students allowed the teachers to learn more about their students and therefore begin to respond on a more personal basis. A family atmosphere developed in the classrooms as a result of the kind of listening and performances that students created around their characters. Quiet students found a way to show their emotional life, and outgoing students developed a way to use words to help them paint their intimate realities. A climate based on mutual respect for each other's work became the norm.

More importantly, high expectations of student performances in the workshop became the natural order of business for the participants and the teachers. These changes were captured in our videotapes of the classes where we could see the growth of students in two dimensions. The students had evolved in their willingness and ability to be physically involved in the characters' representations and more comfortable with the idea of sharing their life experiences through the characters.

Conclusion

The poetry workshop made it possible for me in my role as a University Fellow to find a practical way for putting the UACC reform agenda to work. As a club woman of today

I found it impossible to avoid the mandate of social uplift in Middle School. I was compelled to be an activist on behalf of the least well-served children. More importantly, I was motivated to take action in the Language Arts classrooms, where I was expected to fulfill my responsibility to the UACC and to implement teaching methods that would improve the chances of success among the least well-served African American students. By introducing a kinesthetic approach to teaching Middle School students, I encouraged teachers to look for ways to ensure that students could demonstrate their understanding of life and be valued for their creative approaches to problem solving.

Kinesthetic learners and poetry. While Gardner (1983), Barbe and Milone (1980), and Reif (1992) encourage us to train teachers to be sensitive to students' learning styles, it is important that we remember that all humans probably learn best by doing. Teachers who are shown a model for incorporating multiple ways of knowing and then encouraged to participate in the activities that lead to these new ways of demonstrating knowledge develop a philosophy of teaching that can inform all of their work with students and their own learning. In such an environment, the ten factors that Delpit advances as a means to successful classrooms for urban children become a greater possibility—a welcoming challenge that teachers can expect to meet successfully. By encouraging this kind of classroom, the activist teacher generates a space for more creative possibilities in learning. By so doing she enhances the chances of success for all students.

The teachers and myself accomplished several of the aims of our ambitious plan by the end of the five-week unit. For example, I brainstormed with teachers before each workshop presentation. The teachers and myself, as artist, presented poems and exercises in character development as participants in the process so that students could learn from our process. We videotaped the classes and plan to do an edited version of the five-week workshop for presentation at APAL meetings and other professional engagements.

This article represents our first concerted effort to review our plans and methods for having developed a common language that attempted to facilitate the arts-based pedagogy in the classrooms. Students who were videotaped had proven successful in demonstrating their understanding of the steps that led them to identify with and perform their characters using the text of the poem. While we did not do public demonstrations of the poetry workshop's successes, we did manage to capture individual student performances on videotape so that the students could review and appreciate their own work. Other classes and teachers could benefit from the performances in each of the grades that were represented by consulting the videotape coverage. I believe that the very fact of having a video camera in the classrooms had prompted the students to take their rehearsals seriously. They did work that they felt was representative of the effort that they were committing to the project of character study through text.

The inspector/University Fellow. The work of the inspector, the person who was responsible for the least well-served African American students in the school, was to ensure that students who were failing in Middle School would be given the support needed to improve their performance at school. The poetry workshop allowed me to work with teachers who were committed to changing their philosophy of teaching so that all of their students would have a better chance of doing well.

Our belief in the potential of students became apparent in the attitudes of the teachers who facilitated the poetry workshop. Their activist stance against sloth and indifference among the students encouraged an atmosphere of cooperation by the workshop participants. They also worked as co-learners with the students and were willing to admit that they were growing in expertise along with the students. The teachers demonstrated their commitment to learning by doing rather than by telling students to listen or complete exercises in their notebooks.

My job as a University Fellow was designed to investigate problems and then implement solutions that would lead to more successes in Middle School. This job provided an opportunity for all the children to have an experience in their classrooms that focused on learning through the arts for five weeks. I was given a platform from which I could make practical inroads in the school's pedagogy and further the uplift agenda of the reform initiative. Like my Black sisters of the club movement of the nineteenth century, I made it possible for Black children to experience success in mainstream literacy. Therefore, school improvement that was aimed at one group of students, the least well-served, allowed other participants in the class to benefit from the new arts-based pedagogy. This arts initiative also paved the way among the three APAL teachers to an increased awareness of the possibilities that drama could afford for enhanced learning opportunities for both teachers and students.

The club woman's agenda. The club woman of the nineteenth century may have been primarily committed to the uplift of her sisters who were just out of slavery. They did this work under the yoke of severely constrained financial and social circumstances. Today, working under similar constraints, the activist/teacher/artist has to do similar work in her community. The improvement of the chances of children of color in our Eurocentric male-dominated culture is even more urgent because the odds of failure have increased, and the support systems are being taxed beyond endurance (Edelman, 1984).

Our work, as sisters of the club, is to shore up the shaky scaffolding that is allowing many of our students to fall through the cracks that a neglected infrastructure has allowed for far too long. We, club women and teachers alike, must begin to put into action the kind of commitment that Delpit (Kozol, Wells, Delpit, Rose, Fruchter, Kohl, Meier, & Cole, 1997) describes in her call to President Clinton on behalf of the children. All of us in the role of educators must "value the children . . . protect them . . . care. We all can."

The arts allow us to create safe spaces for children. They allow us to admit to our humanity and thereby potentially make us free to create a world that is inclusive of all voices. In this universe, children come to value the ways in which they are made to feel visible and respected. They then take those habits of thinking and being into their daily lives and improve their chances of success as human beings. If we must be activists who take "direct vigorous action" (*Merriam-Webster*, 1993) against a way of educating that leaves children of color invisible and marginalized, let us do so in the spirit of the Black club women who inspire our creative imaginations. Let us be active in the way of forging bonds in our community that change circumstances to increase the growth of all of our students.

Note

1. Lisa Delpit, 1998, principal investigator of the UACC, personal conversation.

References

Baker, J. (2002). Trilingualism. In L. Delpit & J. K. Dowdy (Eds.), *The skin that we speak: Thoughts on language and culture in the classroom* (pp. 49–62). New York: The New Press.

Barbe, W. & Milone, Jr., M. N. (1980, January). Modality. *Instructor*, 44–49.

Batker, C. (1998). "Love me like I like to be": The sexual politics of Hurston's *Their eyes were watching god*, the classic blues, and the black women's club movement. *African American Review*, 32 (2), 199–213.

Bloom, B. S. (1971). *Handbook on formative and summative evaluation of student earning.* New York: McGraw-Hill Book Company.

Cooper, A. J. (1892). *A voice from the south.* Xenia, Ohio: the Aldine Printing House.

Delpit, L. (2002). No kinda sense. In L. Delpit & J. K. Dowdy (Eds.), *The skin that we speak: Thoughts on language and culture in the classroom* (pp. 31–48). New York: The New Press.

Delpit, L. (1995). *Other people's children: Cultural conflict in the classroom.* New York: New Press.

Dowdy, J. (1999). Becoming the poem: How poetry can facilitate working across differences in a classroom. The change agent. *Adult Education for Social Justice: News, Issues, and Ideas.* MA: Literacy Resource Center.

Dowdy, J. K. (2002). Ovuh Dyuh. In L. Delpit & J. K. Dowdy (Eds.), *The skin that we speak: Thoughts on language and culture in the classroom.* (pp. 3–14). New York: The New Press.

Dowdy, J. K, Givens, G., Murillo Jr., E. G., Shenoy, D., & Villenas, S. (2000). Noises in the attic: The legacy of expectations in the academy. *International Journal of Qualitative Studies in Education*, 13(5), 429–446.

Edelman, M. W. (1984). Black children in America. *The state of Black America 1999.* Image Partners Custom Publishing: National Urban League.

Gardner, H. (1983). *Frames of mind.* New York: Basic Books.

Georgia Public Education Report card, 1999–2000. http://www1.ccboe.net/636.pdf

Giddings, P. (1984). *When and where I enter: The impact of black women on race and sex in America.* New York: Bantam Books.

Harste, J. (1994). Visions of literacy. *Indiana Media Journal, 17*(1), 27-32.

Higginbotham, E. B. (1993). *Righteous discontent: The women's movement in the black Baptist church: 1880-1920*. Cambridge, MA: Harvard University Press.

Kaufman, J. (1999). "Hello, can you play?": Life's roles with puppet performances. In C. T. P. Diamond & C. A. Mullen (Eds.), *The postmodern educator: Arts-based inquiries and teacher development* (pp. 397-407). New York, NY: Peter Lang.

King, N. (1981). From literature to drama to life. In N. McCaslin (Ed.), *Children and drama* (pp. 164-177). New York: Longman Inc.

Kozol, J., Wells. A. S., Delpit, L. D., Rose, M., Fruchter, N., Kohl, H., Meier, D. W., & Cole, R. (1997). Saving public education. *The Nation, 264*(6), 16-25.

Ladson-Billings, G. (2002). 'I ain't writing nuttin': Permissions to fail and demands to succeed in urban classrooms. In L. Delpit & J. K. Dowdy (Eds.), *The skin that we speak: Thoughts on language and culture in the classroom* (pp. 107-120). New York: The New Press.

Lederer, H. (1981). The play's the thing: The use of theater in language teaching. In *Studies in Language Learning, 3*, 35-41.

Lerner, G. (Ed.). (1973). *Black women in white America: A documentary history*. New York: Random House.

Merriam-Webster's Collegiate Dictionary. Springfield, MA: Merriam-Webster.

Meyers, B., Dowdy, J., & Paterson, P. (2000). Finding the missing voices: Perspectives of the least visible families and their willingness and capacity for school involvement. *Current Issues in Middle Level Education, 7*(2), 59-79.

Obidah, J. E. (1999). First year documentation and evaluation report of the Urban Atlanta Coalition Compact. Atlanta, Georgia: Georgia State University, Alonzo A. Crim Center for Educational Excellence.

Painter, N. I. (1996). *Sojourner Truth: A life, a symbol*. New York: W. W. Norton & Co.

Perkins, L. M. (1980). Black women and the philosophy of "race uplift" prior to emancipation. Working paper. National Institute of Education (ED), Washington, DC. (ERIC Document Reproduction Service No. ED 221 444).

Reiff, J. C. (1992). *Learning styles: What research says to the teacher*. Washington, DC: National Education Association.

Robinson, L. C. (2001). France Ellen Watkins Harper.http://www.africana.com/Articles/tt_289.htm

Short, K. G., Harste, J. C., & Burke, C. (1996). *Creating classrooms for authors and inquirers*. Portsmouth, NH: Heinemann.

Woodson, C. G. (1994). *The mis-education of the Negro*. Newport News: United Brothers and Sisters Graphics and Printing.

Contributors

Lisa Delpit is a MacArthur Fellow and recipient of numerous national awards; Delpit was the Principal Investigator for the UACC. She received the award for Outstanding Contribution to Education in 1993 from Harvard Graduate School of Education, which hailed her as a "visionary scholar and woman of courage." She is the author of *Other People's Children: Cultural Conflict in the Classroom* (1995) which received 3 national book awards, and co-author of *The Real Ebonics Debate*, and *The Skin that We Speak*. She is currently the Executive Director/Eminent Scholar of the Center for Urban Education & Innovation at Florida International University, Miami, Florida.

Folami Prescott-Adams who was the director of the Urban Atlanta Coalition Compact, the Atlanta site of the Annenberg Challenge, is a community psychologist and president of Helping Our Minds Expand, Inc. (HOME). HOME is a grassroots organization founded in 1991 and created to provide curriculum development, evaluation and technical support to schools and organizations serving youth and families. She has spent the last 10 years working in school reform. She is currently evaluation director for Communities in Schools of Atlanta. Her works-in-progress include a book based on her research on Parental Mediation of TV Viewing (featured on Cable in the Classroom's web site); Praise Songs and Every Day Songs; The Remix, a compilation of original children's songs; and a thought-provoking media project that incorporates her performance, television production and training talents.

Betty L. Strickland was the Leadership Coach for the UACC. She was the Acting superintendent for the Atlanta Public School System during the inception and first year of UACC, after having served as a teacher, principal, Curriculum Specialist, and Deputy Superintendent for APS. She has received numerous national awards for her leadership in various arenas and was featured on National TV as an outstanding principal who had made a difference in the academic achievement of disenfranchised children.

Chinwe Obijiofor is the mother of five children and a Reading Specialist with a large metropolitan public school system, who at the time she participated in UACC was a first grade teacher. Chinwe was the chairperson of the UACC leadership/action team at her school. She was, at that time and still is, a teacher/consultant for an urban writing project. She has presented her work at a number of local, state, and national educational conferences.

Joan T. Wynne, a former high school English teacher, is an Associate Director of the Center for Urban Education & Innovation and a Professor of Educational Leadership at Florida International University in Miami. She taught at Morehouse College for 14 years, where she designed and directed The Benjamin E. Mays Teacher Scholars Program. She also co-designed and directed an Urban Teacher Leadership Master's Degree Program at Georgia State University. Her research and publishing include issues concerning the instruction of urban children and the impact of racism in schools. She received "The MLK Torch of Peace Award for the Promotion of Racial Harmony" in 2001.

Martha Abbott-Shim, Professor Emeritus of Georgia State University, is the Executive Director of Quality Counts, Inc., a non-profit corporation in support of research and evaluation in the field of early childhood education. Her expertise includes both the developmental assessment of young children and the evaluation of early childhood classroom learning environments and teaching practices. She received her M.Ed. in Tests and Measurement from Boston University and her Ph.D. in Behavioral Sciences from the University of Michigan.

Barbara Meyers is an Associate Professor of Early Childhood Education at Georgia State University. She is Co-director of the Education Specialist Program and Co-editor of The Journal of the Southeastern Regional Association of Teacher Educators. Her research about educational reform in both public and higher education includes shared decision-making, student support teams, family involvement and teacher development. Dr. Meyers received her doctorate from Temple University.

Patricia Paterson is Director of Teacher Quality Initiatives in the P-16 Office of the Board of Regents, University System of Georgia. Her extensive K-12 experience has led to her research interests in reading instruction and in culturally diverse schools. She currently directs programs for recruiting and preparing second-career individuals to teach in high-need schools and for improving teacher working conditions. She holds a Ph.D. in Language and Literacy Education from Georgia State University.

Tracy Woodhall teaches reading and language arts at Carl G. Renfroe Middle School in Georgia. She has a Masters degree in Reading and Literacy. She uses art in the classroom to enhance student motivation and involvement with narrative and expository text.

Lynn Briggs, who was awarded National Board Certification in Early Adolesence English Language Arts, is the Teacher Support/Coach at Carl G. Renfroe Middle School in Decatur, Georgia. She has been teaching language arts and reading since 1990 in middle and high schools, and has also taught math, social studies, and science in middle school. She is committed to using the arts, the community, and the classroom to empower students to know themselves through literature and writing.

Florence Hardney-Hinds has most recently taught ESOL (English to Speakers of Other Languages) in the Cobb County School District in Georgia. She hails from a multicultural background and was raised in Austria, Germany and Japan. Florence has worked as an arts educator at the Metropolitan Museum of Art. For the last 11 years, she has been teaching in a middle school and high school as a Language Arts/Reading/Literature teacher.

Joanne Kilgour Dowdy is an Associate Professor of Adolescent/Adult Literacy at Kent State University in the department of Teaching, Leadership, and Curriculum and Instruction. Her major research interests include women and literacy, drama in education, and video technology in qualitative research instruction.

Professor Baffour Amankwatia II (Asa G. Hilliard III) is the Fuller E. Callaway Professor of Urban Education at Georgia State University. An Educational Psychologist and historian specializing in Ancient African civilizations, he has published widely on African history and culture, powerful schools and teachers, public policy and child growth and development. He has also worked extensively in forensic psychology, testifying in landmark federal cases on IQ, aptitude and achievement test validity.

He is the former Dean of Education at San Francisco State University, and has lectured at many of the major institutions of higher education in the United States, Europe, the West Indies, and the Pacific Islands.

Index

Abbott-Shim, M., ix, xiv
Achievement gap, xi
Action Teams, 8, 9, 108
Adler, E., xvii, xx
African American families
  community-generated solutions for, 98–100
  community involvement activities, 95–98
  community perceptions and, 94–95
  involvement in education, 89
  research about education and, 91–92, 92–94
  school transition and, 90–91
African American students
  academic failure and, 74
  effective schools for, 62
  expectations of, 65
  IQ testing and, 61
  kinesthetic learners, poetry, and, 123
  language arts and, 111–12
  racism and, 66
  statistics, 60, 92, 109
  teacher perceptions of, 71, 77, 79
  teaching drama to, 108
  teaching poetry to, 110, 112–13, 113–17, 117–20, 120–22
  whole language approach and, 76
Aid for Dependent Children, 32
American Educational Research Association, ix

Angelou, M., 83, 84
Annenberg Challenge, xi, 13, 14, 15
Annenberg, W., 14
Armento, B., 91
Atlanta Challenge: Urban Atlanta Coalition Compact, 43
Atlanta Partnership for Arts in Learning, 111, 112, 113, 123
Atlanta Public School System, 31
Avery, M., 58, 59, 63, 64, 66, 74, 80, 83
A Voice from the South (Cooper), 106

Baker, H. J., 91, 108
Barbe, W., 123
Bartolome, L. I., 64
Batker, C., 106
Becker, H. J., 89
Bell Curve (Herrenstein), xix, 61
Berliner, D., xix
Bethune, M. M., 105, 106
Bias in Mental Testing (Jensen), xix
Billig, S., 89, 90
Bloom, B. S., 118
Blyth, D., 91
Bradley Foundation, xix
Branch, T., 82
Briggs, L., ix, xiv
Bronfenbrenner, U., 90
Brown, H. Q., 105
Bullard, A., xvii, xviii, xix

Burke, C., 120
Burroughs, N., 106

Carruthers, J. H., 65
Center for Urban Educational Excellence, 38, 42
Channel One, xx
Chavkin, 100
Christianson, S. L., 89
Churchill, W., 38
Clark, J. H., xviii, 90
Clark, S., 56, 82
club women, 124
Coca-Cola Foundation, 12
Cole, R., 124
collaboration, 5, 18, 105–106
Comer, J., x, 9, 10, 89
Consistency Management and Cooperative Discipline (CMCD), xvi
Cooper, A. J., 105, 106
Coppin, F. J., 105
Corbin, J., 94
Crim, A. A., xi, xii, 8, 36, 81
Crucible, 59, 60
Cubberly, E. P., xix
Culture Matters (Harrison), xix, xx
culture wars, xx

Dauber, S. L., 89, 91
Davies, D., 90, 100, 101
Delpit, L., ix, xi, xiii, xx, 1–10, 12, 13, 15, 38, 63, 71, 72, 73, 74, 79, 80, 81, 107, 108, 111, 122, 123, 124
Dowdy, J. K., ix, xii, xiii, xiv, xx, 90, 100, 109, 110, 117, 122
Dunbar, R. L., 111

Early, S. J., 105
Edison Project, xx
Educate the World, 60, 81
Educational Expo, 75
Educational Leadership, 65
Educational Policy Research Institute, 63
Education Week, 61
Elias, M. J., 90, 91
Epstein, J. L., 89, 91, 100

Fantuzzo, J., 89, 91, 100
Feagin, J., 67, 80
Felner, R., 90, 91
Fine, M., 90, 101
Fisher, A., 18
Fonda, Foundation, 111
Freire, P., 82
Fruchter, N., 124

Gardner, H., 123
Georgia Public Education Report Card, 92, 109
Georgia State University, 38
Giddings, P., 106
Giovanni, N., 111
Givens, G., 122
Goals 2000: Educate America Act, 90
Green, J. S., 111
Green, R. W., 90, 91
Gregory, A., 14
Guba, E., 93

Hamer, F. L., 56
Hampton Negro Conference, 106
Hardney-Hinds, F., ix, xiv
Harper, F. E. W., 105
Harste, J., 120
Harris, L. C., 65
Harvard Educational Review, 59
Henderson, S., 91
Henry, M. E., 90
Heritage Foundation, xix
Higginbotham, E. B., 106
Hilliard, A., 3, 10, 23, 62, 63, 79, 81, 83, 84
Hoover-Dempsey, K. V., 89, 90, 100
Hoover, H. D., 61
Hugar, T., xiv, xvi, xvii
Hughes, L., 111
Hughes, M. F., 63
Hunter, A., xiv

Individualized Education Plan, 16
industrial education, xi
invisible families, 100
Iowa Test of Basic Skills, 61

IQ and the Wealth of Nations (Lynn), xix
Irvine, 79

Jenkins desegregation case, xviii
Jensen, A., xix

King, M. L. Jr., 85
Knoff, H., 89
Kohl, H., 124
Kozol, J., 124
Kuehne, V. S., 89
Kuriloff, P., 90, 101

Ladson-Billings, G., 79, 119
Lareau, A., 101
leadership, 5, 6–7
    capacity-building of, 43–44
    professional development and, 31
Lederer, H., 111
Lerner, G., 106
Levin, D. U., 62, 76
Lincoln, Y., 93

Macedo, D., 64
Mays, B. E., xi
McAdoo, H., 90, 100, 101
McCaleb, S. P., 90
McGrath, D. J., 90, 101
McIntosh, P., 63
Meier, D. W., 124
Menacker, J., 90
mentoring, 41
Meyers, B., ix, xii, xiii, 90, 100, 109
Miller, A., 60
Milne, A. A., 117
Milone Jr., M. N., 123
Moles, O. C., 90
Moorehouse College, xi
Morrison, T., 59, 61
Murray, C., xix, 61
Murillo, E. G. Jr., 122

National Commission on Children, 90
New Horizons, 34
Nobles, W., 70, 79
No Child Left Behind, xix

No Excuses (Thernstrom), xix

Obidah, J. E., 107
Obijiofor, C., ix, 45
Ollendick, T. H., 90, 91
Open Court, xv
Other People's Children (Delpit), ix, 38, 74, 80

Painter, N. I., 119
Parent Teams, 9
Parks, S., 65, 82
Parting the Waters, 82
Paterson, P., ix, xii, xiii, 109
Payne, C., 9
Peachtree Urban Writing Project, 111
Piele, P. K., 39
Piercy, M., 111
Prescott-Adams, F., ix, xiii, 8, 11–30
Principal as Instructional Leader, 37
principals
    alienation among peers, 35
    collaborative leadership and, 35
    dinners, 39–41
    school reform and, 32–33
    strategic planning and, 38
Probst, R. E., 67
professional development, 31, 36–37
Project GRAD, xv

Quality Core Curriculum, 118

racism, 58, 59–65, 67–70, 71–74 76–81
    definition of, 78
    faculty divisiveness and, 72
    institutional, 66
    reverse, 67
    White attitudes and, 84
Raffaele, L., 89
Rich, D., 100
Richards, B., 111
Robinson, L. C., 105
Rokeach, M., 72, 74
Rose, M., 124
Rothstein, R., 61, 62
Rutherford, B., 89, 90

Sandler, H. M., 100
Sankofa Schule, 50
School Power (Comer), x
School Leadership: Handbook for Excellence (Smith), 39
school reform, 105-106
    parent volunteers and, 34
    racism and, 58
    school improvement teams and, 35
Scott, D., xvii
Scriven, M., ix
Shenoy, D., 122
Short, K. G., 120
Sizemore, B., 62, 79
Slaughter, D. T., 89
Slaughter-DeFoe, D. T., 89
Smith, D., xviii, xx
Smith, S. C., 39
Southern Freedom Movement, 56
Spelman College, xi
Spradley, J. P., 93
Status of Education, 60
Stevenson, D. L., 89, 91
Strauss, A., 93
Strickland, B., ix, 4, 8, 28
Success for All, xv, xx

Tatum, B., 66, 67, 70
Tauheed, L., xviii
Terrell, M. C., 106
treatment gap, xi
Truth, S., 119

UACC Expo, 46, 50, 79
Urban Atlanta Coalition Compact (UACC), xi, xii, 1, 3, 4, 6, 7, 8, 10, 63, 64, 65, 67, 68, 70, 71, 73, 80, 83, 84, 105, 107-108

Urban Atlanta Coalition Compact *(contd)*
    academic achievement and, 55
    "across-district" workshops and, 46
    action teams and, 52
    affirmation and, 50-51
    benefit to children, 50
    benefit to teachers, 49-50
    empowerment of teachers and, 55
    Folami Prescott-Adams and, 11-30
    funding for, 61-52
    goals of, 48
    leadership skills and, 51
    obstacles to success of, 45-46, 49
    parent programs and, 45-46
    racist attitudes and, 75
    reform efforts by, 31, 32, 54
    student ability levels and, 56
    teacher support of, 48-49
    test scores and, 47-48
    Town Meetings and, 76
    university fellows and, 107, 108, 124

Villenas, S., 122

Walker, E. V. S., 90
Wellman, D., 67
Wells, A. S., 124
Wentzel, K. R., 89
Whitman, W., 111
Whittle, C., xx
Williams, F. B., 105
Williams, P., 65, 78
whole school change, 38
Woodhall, T., ix, xiv
Wynne, J., ix, xx, 68

Young, A., 85

Studies in the Postmodern Theory of Education

General Editors
Joe L. Kincheloe & Shirley R. Steinberg

Counterpoints publishes the most compelling and imaginative books being written in education today. Grounded on the theoretical advances in criticalism, feminism, and postmodernism in the last two decades of the twentieth century, Counterpoints engages the meaning of these innovations in various forms of educational expression. Committed to the proposition that theoretical literature should be accessible to a variety of audiences, the series insists that its authors avoid esoteric and jargonistic languages that transform educational scholarship into an elite discourse for the initiated. Scholarly work matters only to the degree it affects consciousness and practice at multiple sites. Counterpoints' editorial policy is based on these principles and the ability of scholars to break new ground, to open new conversations, to go where educators have never gone before.

For additional information about this series or for the submission of manuscripts, please contact:
> Joe L. Kincheloe & Shirley R. Steinberg
> c/o Peter Lang Publishing, Inc.
> 275 Seventh Avenue, 28th floor
> New York, New York 10001

To order other books in this series, please contact our Customer Service Department:
> (800) 770-LANG (within the U.S.)
> (212) 647-7706 (outside the U.S.)
> (212) 647-7707 FAX

Or browse online by series:
> www.peterlangusa.com